The psychology of perspective and
Renaissance art

The psychology of perspective and Renaissance art

MICHAEL KUBOVY

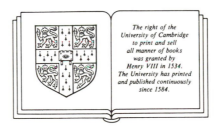

The right of the
University of Cambridge
to print and sell
all manner of books
was granted by
Henry VIII in 1534.
The University has printed
and published continuously
since 1584.

CAMBRIDGE UNIVERSITY PRESS

CAMBRIDGE

LONDON   NEW YORK   NEW ROCHELLE

MELBOURNE   SYDNEY

Published by the Press Syndicate of the University of Cambridge
The Pitt Building, Trumpington Street, Cambridge CB2 1RP
32 East 57th Street, New York, NY 10022, USA
10 Stamford Road, Oakleigh, Melbourne 3166, Australia

First published 1986

Printed in the United States of America

Library of Congress Cataloging in Publication Data
Kubovy, Michael.
The psychology of perspective and Renaissance art.
Bibliography: p.
Includes index.
1. Perspective – Psychological aspects.   2. Visual
perception – Psychological aspects.   3. Painting,
Renaissance – History.   I. Title.
NC750.K85   1986   750′1′8   85-5947
ISBN 0 521 25376 4

British Library Cataloging in Publication applied for

FOR ITAMAR

Contents

vii

Illustrations

ix

xi

Preface

This book is a mixture of psychology and art history. The psychology is based on the large body of research on perception in general and on picture perception in particular. The art history is based on the vast literature on fifteenth-century Italian painting in general and on the development of perspective in particular.

The special character of the book comes from its intention to clarify certain aspects of Renaissance painting by applying some analytic tools of experimental psychology to the paintings of some of its greatest exponents. Since one cannot fruitfully do experiments using these paintings, one must reason by analogy in analyzing these works; thus the style of the book is not in line with most works written by experimental psychologists. It also differs from most works written by art historians, who do not often venture outside the realm of historical documents; when they turn to psychology, they are more likely to appeal to psychoanalysis than to the experimental psychology of perception. The most notable exception is Sir Ernst Gombrich, whose writings are a model to all those who might wish to use the insights of perceptual research to better understand visual art.

The text does not assume any prior knowledge of art history, perceptual theory, or geometry. When I deal with an issue on a level more appropriate to the specialist, the text is set off in brackets:

[This is an example of how I set off certain technical discussions from the rest of the text. It can be omitted without loss of continuity.]

Polemical material I usually relegate to footnotes, unless it is germane to the main thrust of my argument.

I wish to express my gratitude to friends and colleagues for their help in various phases of this project: to Wendell R. Garner, who got the ball rolling by suggesting that I teach a course on the psychology of art at Yale; to Miri Kubovy, who introduced me to art history and was enthusiastic about this project in all its stages; to Samuel Y. Edgerton, Jr., Reni and Marcel Franciscono, Wendell R. Garner, Martin J. Kemp, Miri Kubovy, William and Claire McGuire, Irvin Rock, and Michael Sukale, who made many important, and sometimes crucial, suggestions; to Catherine Randazzo, for her unflagging enthusiasm in dealing with essential technical matters such as permissions; and to Itamar Kubovy, for his excellent technical assistance and for suggesting the best title for the book (which is not the current one). I wish also to acknowledge the support of the U.S. Public Health Service (grants to Yale and to Rutgers universities on "Attention and Pre-Attention in Audition and Vision"), Rutgers University Research Council (grants on "Apparent and Mental Rotation of Three-Dimensional Bodies" and "Dimensions of Similarity and Grouping"), Rutgers University Johanna Busch Memorial Fund (grant on "Attention and Pre-Attention in Audition and Vision"), and to the National Science Foundation (grant on "Visual Imagery, Space, and Pictorial Representation").

M.K.

New York City

The psychology of perspective and
Renaissance art

Figure I-1. Andrea Mantegna,
Archers Shooting at Saint Chris-
topher *(1451–5). Fresco. Ovetari
Chapel, Eremitani Church, Padua.*

Figure I-2. Taddeo Gaddi, The
Presentation of the Virgin *(1332–
8). Fresco. Baroncelli Chapel,
Church of Santa Croce, Florence.*

Introduction: The importance of perspective and the metaphor of the arrow in the eye

There is a frightening detail in Andrea Mantegna's *Archers Shooting at Saint Christopher* (Figure I-1 and jacket illustration) that shows a man who has just been shot through the eye with an arrow. I see the arrow in the eye as a metaphor for the art of perspective; I have reason to believe that Mantegna did so too.

Why would Mantegna want to incorporate a metaphor for the art of perspective into a fresco?

Primarily, he would want to because perspective played a central role among the intellectual and aesthetic concerns of Renaissance artists. Indeed, as we shall see, perspective has been thought to have many aesthetic functions in Renaissance painting. (In this book, I propose yet another, a deliberate discrepancy between the viewer's actual point of view and a virtual point of view experienced by the viewer on the basis of cues contained in the perspectival organization of the painting.)

The most obvious function of perspective was to rationalize the representation of space: With the advent of perspective, it became much easier to stage, as it were, elaborate group scenes organized in a spatially complex fashion. Compare the preperspectival architectural extravaganza to which Taddeo Gaddi was forced to resort in order to define the spatial locations of his figures (Figure I-2), to the simplicity of means used by Piero della Francesca (Figure I-3) to achieve a precise definition of relative spatial locations. Then, of course, perspective gave Renaissance artists the means to produce a compelling illusion

I

Figure I-3. Piero della Francesca,
Flagellation *(probably 1450s).*
Panel. Galleria Nazionale delle
Marche, Palazzo Ducale, Urbino.

of depth. We will come back to this illusion and the psychological research that elucidates it in Chapter 3.

In addition to rationalizing the representation of space and providing an illusion of depth, perspective provided the means for drawing the spectator's eye to the key figure or action in the painting.[1] Take, for instance, Masaccio's *The Tribute Money* (Figure I-4). The slanted lines representing the horizontal features of the building that recede into the distance, called *orthogonals* because they represent lines in the scene that are perpendicular to the picture plane, converge at a point known as the *vanishing point* of this perspective construction (a concept explained in the next chapter). The vanishing point falls just barely to the right of Christ's head, thus drawing attention to the central actor in the drama Masaccio has represented. In Piero della Fran-

---

[1] There is a tendency to think of paintings as the representation of "one intercepted moment, a single instant" (as Steinberg puts it), much like the "freeze frame" technique sometimes used in films. In his analysis of Leonardo's *Last Supper*, Steinberg (1973) has shown the nefariousness of this notion.

2

Figure I-4. Masaccio, Tribute Money *(ca. 1425). Brancacci Chapel, Church of Santa Maria del Carmine, Florence.*

cesca's Brera altarpiece (Figure I-5), the vanishing point coincides with the Madonna's left eye. In Leonardo da Vinci's *Last Supper* (see Figure 8-9), the vanishing point is centered upon Christ's head.

In other cases, such as Domenico Veneziano's *Martyrdom of Saint Lucy* (Figure I-6), the vanishing point coincides with a central locus of the action rather than the head of the main figure: the hand of the executioner that has just plunged a dagger into Saint Lucy's throat. In Raphael's *Dispute Concerning the Blessed Sacrament* (Figure I-7), the vanishing point coincides with the representation of the Host. Or, more subtly, in Piero della Francesca's *Flagellation* (Figure I-3), the scourge, held by the man immediately to the right of Christ's figure in the picture, is related to the system of orthogonals that recede into the distance. Even though the scourge is vertical and is not itself an orthogonal, its extension passes through the vanishing point.

One should not, however, expect the vanishing point in Renaissance paintings always to coincide with an element that is important to the narrative: Sometimes the vanishing point interacts with the more visual elements of the painting, such as in Domenico Veneziano's *Madonna and Child with Four Saints* (Figure I-8), in which the folds of the Madonna's cloak form a triangular pattern as it drapes between her knees. The downward-pointing vertex

3

Figure I-5. Piero della Francesca, Madonna and Child, Six Saints, Four Angels, and Duke Federico II da Montefeltro *(Brera altarpiece) (ca. 1472–4). Panel. Pinacoteca di Brera.*

of this triangle (which is echoed in the decoration between the arches) is also the vanishing point of the perspective. It should be noticed, however, that Domenico uses the fan of orthogonals to organize many important features of the painting, just as Piero did with the scourge in the *Flagellation*. For instance, the eyes of Saint Francis (the figure on the left) fall upon an orthogonal; the left eye of Saint John (the second figure from the left) and the tips of the thumb and the index finger of his right hand fall on an orthogonal; the right eye of Saint Zenobius (the second figure from the right) and the tips of his index and middle fingers are

4

Figure I-6. Domenico Veneziano, Martyrdom of Saint Lucy *(ca. 1445). Panel. Gemäldegalerie, West Berlin.* ▶

Figure I-7. Raphael, Dispute Concerning the Blessed Sacrament *(1509). Fresco. Stanza della Segnatura, Vatican, Rome.* ▼

Figure I-8. Domenico Veneziano, Madonna and Child with Four Saints, *also known as* La Sacra Conversazione *(Saint Lucy altarpiece) (ca. 1445). Panel. Galleria Uffizi, Florence.*

also aligned on an orthogonal. In other cases, the vanishing point falls on a point in a distant background landscape, such as in Pietro Perugino's *Virgin Appearing to Saint Bernard* (Figure I-9).

To these three uses of perspective (the illusionistic, narrative focus, and structural focus) Warman Welliver has recently added a fourth: "The new rules of perspective drawing gave to the painter and relief sculptor . . . a new code for concealing allusion and meaning in his work." He shows how perspective enabled Domenico Veneziano and Piero della Francesca to translate the floor plans of complex buildings – the architectural dimensions and proportions of which bore allegorical or symbolic significance – into painting. Here is his analysis of certain aspects of Domenico's *Sacra Conversazione* (Figure I-8).

The most obvious factor in Domenico's scheme of dimensions and proportions, as might be expected, is three. The elemental shape from which the pattern of floor tiles is derived is the equilateral triangle; the viewing distance, or invisible floor, is three times the visible floor; the Gothic facade consists of three

6

bays and is three G [= the interval between columns of the Gothic loggia] high (including the putative entablature) by three wide; the floor is 9 feet wide at the baseline and the total depth of the architecture beyond the baseline is 27, or 3^3, feet.

A second and less obvious element in the proportions is the interplay between 2 and 3. We look across a floor which is 3/2 G deep at an elevation (without the entablature) of which the base is 2/3 G below eye level and the proportions above eye level are 2:3. The overall proportions of the elevation, 8:9, are equivalent to $2^3:3^2$. The proportions of the four large rectangles of floor into which the plan forward of the exhedra naturally divides are, beginning with the invisible floor, 3:2, 1:2, 1:3, and 2:3.

No doubt the theological allusion of this coupling of 2 and 3 is the expansion of the dual deity to the Trinity with the coming of Christ. (Welliver, 1973, p. 8)

Now Mantegna's interest in perspective was somewhat different from the interests of his contemporaries. He often explored the relation between the virtual space represented in the picture and the real space in which the spectator stood. In the *Martyrdom of Saint James* (Figure I-8), which we will discuss in Chapter I, the head of Saint James ap-

Figure I-9. Pietro Perugino, Virgin Appearing to Saint Bernard *(1488–9). Panel. Alte Pinakothek, Munich.*

7

pears to invade the spectator's real space. I will also show (in Chapter 8) that in *Saint James Being Led to Execution* (Figure 8-7) Mantegna creates a disturbing conflict between the spectator's actual line of sight and the virtual line of sight implied by the painting. These are examples – the detailed discussion of which must be postponed – of Mantegna's adventurous use of perspective.

Having seen how important perspective was for Renaissance art and the central role it played in Mantegna's art, let us now return to Mantegna's *Archers shooting at Saint Christopher*. Two tragedies befell this fresco painted on the wall of the Ovetari Chapel of the Eremitani Church in Padua. By the time it was first photographed in color, during the Second World War, it had deteriorated to such an extent that its bottom third and the figure of the saint on the left were defaced beyond recognition; on March 11, 1944, soon after the fresco was photographed, the entire east end of the church, which contained the Ovetari chapel, was destroyed in an American air raid on the nearby railway yards of Padua. Frederick Hartt writes:

Only pathetically small fragments of Mantegna's frescoes were recovered, and these...are now mounted in the chapel upon frescoes reconstructed from photographs. The reconstruction, however painstaking, gives only an echo of the lost masterpieces. (Hartt, 1969, p. 350)

Fortunately, there exists a copy of the fresco, shown in Figure I-10, which can give us a reading of the parts of the fresco for which no photograph exists. For instance, we can see that Saint Christopher was (as Jacobus of Voragine puts it in his *Golden Legend*, a thirteenth-century compendium of legends about the lives of the saints often consulted by Renaissance artists) "a man of prodigious size, being twelve cubits in height, and fearful of aspect" (Jacobus de Voragine, 1969, p. 377). Jacobus describes the relevant episode of Saint Christopher's martyrdom as follows:

Then the king [of Samos] had him tied to a pillar, and ordered four thousand soldiers to shoot arrows at him. But the arrows hung in mid-air, nor could a single one of them touch Christopher. And when the king, thinking that he was already trans-

8

Figure I-10. Copy after Mantegna, Archers Shooting at Saint Christopher; Saint James Being Led to Execution; Saint Christopher's Body Being Dragged Away after His Beheading. *Collection du Musée Jacquemart-André, Paris.*

fixed with arrows, shouted invectives at him, suddenly an arrow fell from the air, turned upon him, struck him in the eye, and blinded him. Then Christopher said: "I know, O king, that I shall be dead on the morrow. When I am dead, do thou, tyrant, make a paste of my blood, rub it upon thine eyes, and thou shalt recover thy sight!" Then at the king's order he was beheaded; and the king took a little of his blood, and placed it upon his eyes, saying: "In the name of God and Saint Christopher!" And at once he was made whole. Then the king was baptized, and decreed that whoever should blaspheme against God or Saint Christopher should at once be beheaded. (Jacobus de Voragine, 1969, pp. 381–2)

Mantegna's interpretation agrees with Jacobus's account; so at first blush it would seem that Mantegna's representation of the arrow in the eye is traditional and that there is therefore no evidence of a metaphorical role for this aspect of the picture.

However, when one looks for pictorial antecedents for the arrow lodged in the king's eye, one realizes the novelty of Mantegna's interpretation – for there are none. In Italian painting, Saint Christopher – like all the other saints – appears both in isolated images and in cycles depicting the saint's life.[2] Twenty-four isolated images of Saint Christopher have been cataloged, most of which represent him in the act of carrying the Christ-child across a river (whence

[2] See Kaftal's (1952, 1965, 1978) compendia on the iconography of the saints in Italian painting.

9

his name, which means "Christ-bearer"). Only one of them depicts the miracle of the recalcitrant arrows: It is part of a polyptych on various subjects painted by an anonymous Venetian painter between 1325 and 1335.[3] It does not show the arrow in the eye. All seven cycles (including the one to which Mantegna's fresco belongs[4]) contain a scene representing the recalcitrant arrows;[5] but as far as the poor state of preservation of these frescoes allows us to tell, only Mantegna's shows the episode of the arrow in the eye. If this is true, and if we may assume that Renaissance artists did not deviate easily from traditional practice in the representation of scenes from the lives of the saints or from the life of Christ, it suggests that Mantegna may have had good reason for drawing the viewer's attention to the arrow in the eye.

Let us now see what the arrow in the eye may have meant to Renaissance artists. Beyond the observation that rays of light traced from points on an object into the eye suggest arrows penetrating the eye (see Figure 1-2), perspective and arrows were compared in several texts written by Mantegna's contemporaries.

In 1435, about two decades before Mantegna painted the *Archers Shooting at Saint Christopher*, Alberti wrote *On Painting*, which contains the earliest known geometric and optical analysis of linear perspective.[6] After his exposition of perspective he writes:

---

[3] For an illustration, see Pallucchini, 1964, Figure 217.

[4] Not all of which were painted by Mantegna; some were painted by Bono da Ferrara and Ansuino da Forli.

[5] The cycles are all frescoes. In northeastern Italy: Ridolfo Guariento (active 1338–70) in the Church of San Domenico at Bolzano (these frescoes have been destroyed); School of the Veneto (early fifteenth century) in the Church of Santa Lucia (partly ruined); Bertolino dei Grossi (attribution uncertain) between 1417 and 1422 in the Valeri family chapel in the Cathedral at Parma. In Tuscany: Spinello Aretino (ca. 1346–1410) in the Church of San Domenico, Arezzo; Parri Spinelli in the Cathedral at Arezzo.

[6] Leon Battista Alberti (1404–72) was not himself a major painter. He was a playwright, mathematician, lawyer, cartographer, humanist, architect, linguist, and cryptographer – in short, the prototypical Renaissance man. In 1435 and 1436, he published *De pictura* in Latin and *Della pittura* in Italian (Alberti, 1966). See Gadol, 1969.

These instructions are of such a nature that [any painter] who really understands them well both by his intellect and by his comprehension of the definition of painting will realize how useful they are. Never let it be supposed that anyone can be a good painter if he does not clearly understand what he is attempting to do. *He draws the bow in vain who has nowhere to point the arrow.* (Emphasis mine. Alberti, 1966, p. 59)[7]

Because Mantegna had most probably read Alberti's treatise,[8] the arrow in the eye (which represents soldiers who have just drawn the bow in vain) could have been a veiled reference to Alberti's text. Indeed the architecture in the fresco is strongly reminiscent of Alberti's style.[9] For instance, the bridge in *Saint Christopher's Body Being Dragged Away after His Beheading* (Figure I-11) is very similar to the flank of Alberti's Church of San Francesco (the Tempio Malatestiano,[10] Figure I-12). Furthermore, the frieze in Mantegna's fresco that underlines the first floor in which the King of Samos was hit in the eye reminds one of the frieze that serves as a pedestal for the columns of the Tempio Malatestiano's flank (see Figure I-13). In this context, we are also led to notice the similarity between the inscription visible on the facade of Mantegna's building and the inscriptions on the funerary urns on the flank of the Tempio Malatestiano (Figure I-13). Furthermore, there is a resemblance between one of the onlookers watching Saint Christopher's body being dragged away and a portrait of Alberti (compare Figure I-14 to Figure I-15). Finally, the main event taking place in the fresco on the left (the tyrant being hit in the eye by the arrow) is seen through a window. Given all the other evidence that indicates that this

[7] See J. R. Spencer's footnote 52 in Alberti, 1966, p. 117, in which he suggests that the source of this aphorism is in Cicero, *De oratore*, I, xxx, 135; *De finibus*, III, vi, 22.

[8] We know that they met, but we have no evidence that they did before 1460, a few years after the Eremitani frescoes were painted (Puppi, 1974).

[9] This observation was made by Arcangeli (1974) and by Pignatti (1978).

[10] This temple was a "modernization" of the monastic Church of San Francesco in Rimini, which was designed as a temple to the Renaissance tyrant Sigismondo Malatesta, and for which the cornerstone was laid in 1450.

Figure I-11. Andrea Mantegna,
Saint Christopher's Body Being
Dragged Away after His Be-
heading *(1451–5). Fresco. Ovetari
Chapel, Eremitani Church, Padua.*

fresco is an homage to Alberti, the location of this crucial
scene in a window may be a reference to *Alberti's window*,
a central concept in perspective, which Alberti explains as
follows:

First of all, on the surface on which I am going to paint, I draw
a rectangle of whatever size I want, which I regard as an open
window through which the subject to be painted is to be seen.[11]

So if the setting in which this dramatic event is taking place
is Albertian, and the scene of the arrow in the eye is seen,
so to speak, through an Alberti window, then the conjecture that the arrow in the eye is a reference to Alberti's
text becomes plausible.

[11] Quoted by Edgerton (1975, p. 42), from Grayson's (1972) translation.
We will return to this concept in Chapter 1. This key concept is often
unjustly called the Leonardo window (Pirenne, 1970) or da Vinci's pane
(Danto, 1981); it ought to be called *Alberti's window*, after its originator.

12

Figure I-12. Leon Battista Alberti, Church of San Francesco, Rimini (Tempio Malatestiano), west flank (foundation laid 1450).

Figure I-13. Leon Battista Alberti, Church of San Francesco, Rimini (Tempio Malatestiano) view of the west flank, showing frieze and inscription on an urn in one of the niches.

13

Our conjecture gains further support from the existence of a second reference to arrows, in a text by Filarete.[12] In his *Treatise on Architecture*, Filarete discusses the technique of drawing in perspective; much of what he has to say on this topic is an improved exposition of Alberti's ideas. At one point, while he is explaining how to draw square buildings, Filarete writes:

If you wish to make doors, windows, or stairs, everything should be drawn to this point, because, as you have understood, the centric point is your eye,[13] on which everything should rest just as *the crossbowman* always takes his aim on a fixed and given point. [Emphasis mine. Filarete (Antonio di Piero Averlino), 1965, pp. 304–5]

Because the treatise is later than Mantegna's fresco (it was written between 1461 and 1464), Filarete could have borrowed it from Mantegna, from Alberti, or perhaps from yet another source.

It becomes harder yet to believe in a coincidence when we discover that the metaphor also occurs in Leonardo's notebooks. In discussing the question of whether rays of light emanate from the eye or from the bodies that are seen, Leonardo expresses the view that "the eye [is] adapted to receive like the ear the images of objects without transmitting some potency in exchange for these" (Leonardo da Vinci, 1938, p. 251). And then, to support his view, he says:

The circle of the light which is in the middle of the white of the eye is by nature suitable to apprehend objects. This same circle has in it a point which seems black and this is a nerve bored through it which goes within the seat of the powers charged with the power of receiving impressions and forming judgment, and this penetrates to the common sense. Now the objects which are over against the eyes act with the rays of their images *after the manner of many archers who wish to shoot through the bore of a*

Figure I-14. Andrea Mantegna, detail of Figure I-11.

Figure I-15. Leon Battista Alberti, Self-portrait. Samuel H. Kress Collection, National Gallery of Art, Washington.

[12] Filarete is the nom-de-plume of Antonio Averlino (ca. 1400–ca. 1469), a Florentine sculptor and architect.
[13] Filarete seems to be conflating two concepts here: If he is talking about a point in the picture plane, he must be referring to the vanishing point, to which converge the images of lines orthogonal to the picture plane; if he is talking about the eye, he must be referring to the center of projection; see Chapter 1.

14

carbine, for the one among them who finds himself in a straight line with the direction of the bore of the carbine will be most likely to touch the bottom of this bore with his arrow; so the objects opposite to the eye will be more transferred to the sense when they are in line with the transfixing nerve. (Emphasis mine. Leonardo da Vinci, 1938, p. 252)

Every technical field develops certain stock images that are proven pedagogical tools. It would be a very unlikely coincidence if three authors used the arrow-in-the-eye metaphor in discussing perspective and optics unless it had become part of the imagery involved in thinking about perspective, a metaphor they lived by.[14]

But if a small circle of experts lived by this metaphor, could Mantegna expect his audience to read this undeclared rebus? I believe so. Puzzles and esoteric allusions were a pervasive feature of Florentine art. Renaissance Florentines, for all their interest in geometry and mathematics, should by no means be considered to be rationalists in the post-Cartesian sense. Indeed, shortly after Mantegna painted the frescoes in the Ovetari Chapel, in 1460, Marsilio Ficino (1433–99), a priest, the founder of the Platonic Academy in Florence, and one of the quattrocento's most influential philosophers, translated part of the Hermetic literature, a collection of treatises concerned with astrology, alchemy, and other occult sciences, written between A.D. 100 and 300. The text appears to have filled a need and gained a wide readership. As Welliver says:

One very strong manifestation of the tendency of Florentine art to be intellectual was the Florentine penchant for the subtle and the esoteric. The Florentine artist or poet frequently spoke a much different message to the initiate from that received by the profane; indeed it would hardly be an exaggeration to say that the most typical kind of Florentine work was a riddle concealed from the profane by the trappings of innocence. This was a tradition sanctified by the example of Dante and increasingly

[14] To borrow the felicitous title of Lakoff and Johnson's (1981) book. Arrows seem also to play a major role in technical illustrations of Alberti's writings on architecture. See, for example, Plate XI in Alberti, 1955. Hatfield and Epstein (1979, Figure 2, p. 374) reproduce an illustration of the visual system from a 1664 edition of Descartes's *L'homme* in which an arrow represents a generalized object.

15

reinforced, throughout the fifteenth century, by the rediscovery of Plato. It was the consistent element in Florentine nature which impelled the observant Jew from abroad, Joachim Alemanni, to write in 1490 that no people had ever been so given to communication by parable and riddle as the Florentines. (Welliver, 1973, p. 20)

It should be noted that these observations can legitimately be generalized to include the artists of Padua as well, because many artists of Florentine origin were active in the North (Gentile da Fabriano and Pisanello in Venice; Andrea del Castagno in San Zaccaria; Filippo Lippi, Paolo Uccello, and especially Donatello in Padua).

Thus, by showing that the arrow in the eye may have been a commonly used metaphor in Renaissance artistic circles, and that esoteric references were common in Renaissance art, we support our claim that Mantegna's audience would appreciate a subtle reference to perspective in a painting.

The thesis of this book is that there is yet another role for perspective in Renaissance art. It is a subtle role, having to do with the spectator's experience of his or her location in space with respect to the physical surface of the painting and with respect to the room in which the painting is viewed. I will show in the following chapters that Renaissance painters deliberately induced a discrepancy between the spectator's *actual* point of view and the point of view from which the scene is *felt* to be viewed. The result is a spiritual experience that cannot be obtained by any other means. So, whether or not Mantegna intended the arrow in the eye to draw the spectator's attention to the deeper significance of perspective, I hope this book will.

1   The elements of perspective

Here the total artifice reveals itself
As the total reality.
>Wallace Stevens, from "Someone Puts a Pineapple
>Together," 1947 (Stevens, 1972, p. 299)

Look at Masaccio's *Trinity* (Figure 1-1), the oldest surviving painting that uses perspective rigorously. Why it looks compellingly three-dimensional will be explained in Chapter 3. In this chapter, we will discuss the geometry that underlies perspective; in Chapter 2, we will look at the origins of perspective.

We, in the late twentieth century, take photography for granted as the prototypical physical embodiment of picture taking, and perspective as its mathematical model. But for the artists–scientists of the Renaissance the introduction of perspective required a complex mesh of innovations: They had to define the very concept of taking a picture, to understand the optics implied by this definition, to abstract the geometry underlying the optics, and finally to discover ways of translating these abstractions into practical rules of thumb that anyone could apply in order to draw scenes in perspective. In the Introduction, we have already encountered Alberti's description of his key concept of taking a picture. Let me quote it again:

First of all, on the surface on which I am going to paint, I draw a rectangle of whatever size I want, which I regard as an open window through which the subject to be painted is to be seen. (See Figure 1-2)

17

Before we analyze the relation between the Alberti window and perspective, a distinction must be made between the study of perspective as the theory of picture taking and the practice of drawing in perspective. In the remainder of this chapter, we will deal mostly with the theory of per-

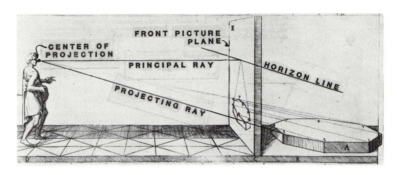

Figure 1-2. Representation of Alberti's window (perspective drawn using a front picture plane). Engraving (modified) from G.B. Vignola, La due regole della prospettiva practica, 1611.

spective, that is, with the nature of the geometric transformation that allows us to represent a three-dimensional scene on a two-dimensional surface, and with certain features that all perspective representations have in common. After presenting these notions in some detail, we will dwell briefly on the procedure that Alberti invented, but because this is a very complicated topic to which numerous textbooks have been devoted, the reader should not expect to learn from this book how to draw a perspectively correct representation.[1]

Perspective is easiest to understand once we are familiar with the *camera obscura* ("dark chamber" in Latin) illustrated in Figures 1-3 and 1-4. Although the issue is shrouded in uncertainty, there is some evidence that the device was invented by Alberti (Pastore and Rosen, 1984). It is no more than a box, or a room, with a relatively small hole in it, called a *pinhole*. If the box is to serve its purpose as a *camera obscura*, light should not enter it except through the pinhole. The side of the box opposite the pinhole is called the *picture plane*. If the picture plane is painted white and all the other sides are lined with light-absorbing black velvet, we can be sure that all the light that falls on the picture plane has traveled in a straight line from an object outside the box through the pinhole and that none of it has been reflected from the walls. So, moving into geometry, a *camera obscura* creates an image x of an object point v by ensuring that one and only one ray of light, called a *projecting ray*, coming from v hits the picture plane at x after passing through the pinhole. Unless the *camera*

---

[1] I have found Gill (1974, 1975) very useful in this regard.

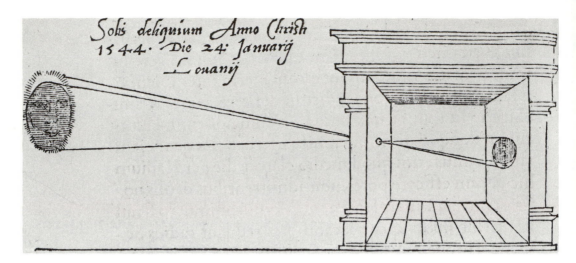

Figure 1-3. Earliest known illustration of a camera obscura. Engraving from R. Gemma Frisius, De radio astronomico et geometrico liber, 1545. The legend translates: "Observing solar eclipse of 24 January 1544."

obscura is a room in which a spectator can stand and look at the picture plane (in which case the picture will be both large and very faint), we must devise a way of showing the picture it takes. There are two ways to do that: Either replace the wall of the picture plane with a piece of ground glass and view the image from outside, or replace it with a photosensitive plate that can be developed into a photograph. In the latter case, we will have a pinhole camera, that is, a photographic camera with a pinhole for a lens.[2]

[The main drawback of the pinhole camera is the dimness of the image it creates. If one enlarges the aperture, the image becomes blurred. In modern cameras, lenses are used to focus the light coming in through a relatively large aperture, thus assuring a sharply defined image.]

A *camera obscura* does not correspond exactly to Alberti's window, for it inverts right for left and top for bottom (as Figure 1-3 shows). To understand the basis of perspective as discovered by Alberti, consider Figure 1-5: We project a point M onto a point m on a front picture plane (P), replacing the pinhole with a *center of projection* (O), and replacing the optical process underlying the *camera obscura* with a geometric transformation called *central projection*. It is essential to keep in mind that the scheme of central projection is a convenient geometric fiction: No optical

---

[2] The pinhole camera and fascinating experiments using it are described in Pirenne (1970). (See also Hammond, 1981, and Kitao, 1980.)

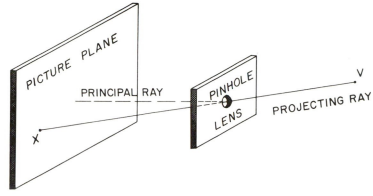

Figure 1-4. Geometry of the camera obscura

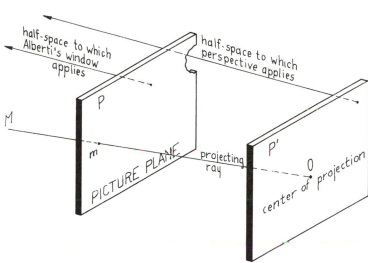

Figure 1-5. Main features of central projection

system can be devised to perform such a transformation in this way.[3] Because central projection is a geometric abstraction, it can be misleading to link it too closely with vision – which *is* based on an optical process – as textbooks almost invariably do. It is better, I believe, to first comprehend perspective as a purely geometric procedure for the representation of a three-dimensional world on a two-dimensional surface before one tries to understand its perceptual effects on viewers. One should avoid thinking of it as a method that mimics, in some sense, what we see.

[3] Such a projection onto a front picture plane would be physically realizable only by a two-stage optical process: The first stage would essentially be a *camera obscura*, projecting a scene onto a rear picture plane, which produces an upside-down picture, and then projecting the upside-down picture again to produce an upright picture.

21

We will see later (Chapter 3) that there is a sense in which a perspective representation mimics what could be seen from a certain point of view, but I have found it useful to postpone that interpretation of perspective and to consider it in the course of an exploration of the reasons why a perspective picture looks compellingly three-dimensional (see Chapter 3). The traditional representation of Figure 1-2, which places an eye at the center of projection and calls the center of projection the "vantage point" or the "station point," is a convenient pedagogical device – except that it takes the step of relating vision to central projection before the purely geometric nature of the transformation is made clear.

Up to this point, we have been talking as if central projection and perspective were the same. The truth is that central projection is a somewhat more general geometric transformation than perspective. In central projection, one defines (see Figure 1-5) a picture plane P and a center of projection O (which is not contained in the plane P). The central projection of any point M (distinct from O) is the point m, which is the intersection of the projecting ray OM with the plane P. It is important to keep in mind that this definition does not restrict the location of M with respect to P: It could be anywhere in space relative to the picture plane – in front of it or behind it. Now because perspective is a model of the picture-taking process, it restricts itself to a 180-degree field of view from the vantage point of O, pointing toward the picture plane. That is why perspective applies only to the projection of points M contained in the half-space (an infinite region of space bounded by a surface) that contains the picture plane P and that is bounded by a plane P' that contains the center of projection O and is parallel to the picture plane P. This much constraint upon the geometry is imposed by the optical nature of the phenomenon we are trying to model: The maximum field of a pinhole camera is 180 degrees. This formulation of perspective is still somewhat more general than Alberti's window, which implies that only objects *behind* the window can be projected onto the picture plane. Indeed, in the large majority of the cases, perspective is restricted to the region beyond the window.

There are two ways of formulating this point, geometric and perceptual. Geometrically speaking, the points M are limited to the closed half-space which does not contain O, and is bounded by the picture plane, P (see Figure 1-5). The geometric evidence for this point can be found in the size of the depictions of known objects. The geometry of perspective implies that the painting of an object which is in front of the picture plane will be larger-than-life; since Renaissance painters very rarely painted larger-than-life figures, most figures must be behind the picture plane.[4]

Psychologically speaking, most pictures look as if they were seen through a window – none of the objects seems to pop out into the space of the room; the scenes they depict appear to be entirely behind the surface of the painting. The evidence for this psychological observation comes from the exception to this rule. In these rare exceptions, we see the lengths to which an artist must go to coax the spectator into relinquishing the assumption that the entire scene is behind a window. Take for instance an anonymous illumination of the twelfth century (Figure 1-6). Because the fish occludes part of the frame, we assume that it is flying in front of the page. But to attribute this perceptual effect to the occlusion of a section of the frame implies that, in the absence of this device, the scene would be perceived to be entirely beyond the page. In other words, even in preperspectival pictorial representations, we tend to perceive a picture frame as the frame of a window through which we can look into the virtual space depicted by the picture. One of the most brilliant applications of this method is in Jan van Eyck's *Annunciation* (Figure 1-7). In this diptych,[5] we see the angel and Mary represented in a grey simulation of figures sculpted in the round, standing on octagonal pedestals. Behind them, just touching the far

---

[4] "You must make the foremost figure in the picture less than the size of nature in proportion to the number of braccia at which you place it from the front line . . . " (Leonardo da Vinci, 1970, §538, p. 324).

[5] A diptych is a pair of painted panels hinged together.

23

ıuıtas ſyrie que nunc tyrus dıcat̃. olım
ſerra uocabat̃ a pıſce quodam quı ıllıc
abundabat. quem ſua lıngua ſar apellat̃
ex quo derıuatũ eſt huiˀ ſımılıtudınıſ pıſ/
cıculos ſardas. ſardınaſ   q̃ uocarı.

Figure 1-6. The Flying Fish of
Tyre *(ca. 1170). Ms. 81, the Pier-*
pont Morgan Library, New York.

surface of the pedestals, we see a black mirrorlike surface
in which the statues appear to be reflected, framed by dark
moldings, part of which are occluded by the angel's left
wing and by Mary's cloak.

It is possible to achieve the same effect by propagation,
that is, to have object *A* occlude the frame, and to suggest
(whether by occlusion or other means) that object *B* is in
front of object *A:* The result is that object *B* seems to be
in front of the picture plane. Such is one of the interesting
perspective effects used by Mantegna in his frescoes for
the Ovetari Chapel (Figure 1-8). In the *Martyrdom of Saint
James,* the railing appears to be attached to the front of the
picture frame; that is why the torso of the soldier leaning
over it appears to emerge into the space of the chapel,
above the floor onto which Saint James's head will roll
when it is severed.

24

Figure 1-7. Jan van Eyck, Annunciation (after 1432). Thyssen-Bornemisza Collection, Lugano, Switzerland.

Figure 1-8. Mantegna, Martyrdom of Saint James *(1451–5). Fresco. Ovetari Chapel, Eremitani Church, Padua.*

Returning now to our exposition of the elements of perspective, there are three geometric properties of central projection that we must understand in order to proceed with our analysis of the psychology of perspective.

Proposition 1. The perspectival image of a straight line that does not pass through the center of projection is always a straight line (the image of a straight line that does pass through the center of projection, i.e., of a projecting ray, is a point).

The second property of perspective concerns the representation of sets of parallel lines (such as you would have to contend with in drawing a box). First, consider a set of vertical lines. If the picture plane is not vertical, the images of all vertical lines converge onto the one and only *vertical vanishing point.* Figure 1-9 illustrates this property as it occurs in a picture of a box projected onto a picture plane tilted sharply downward. Next, consider a set of horizontal lines. They too converge onto a vanishing point. To specify the location of this vanishing point, we must first define

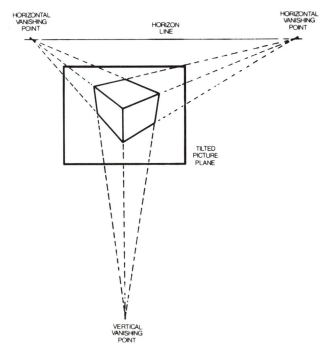

Figure 1-9. *Vanishing points*

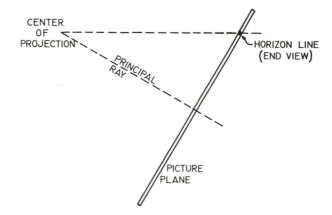

CENTER
OF
PROJECTION

PRINCIPAL
RAY

HORIZON LINE
(END VIEW)

PICTURE
PLANE

Figure 1-10. Definition of the horizon line

the *horizon line* of the picture (see Figure 1-10), which is the line defined by the intersection of the picture plane (which need not be vertical) and a horizontal plane that contains the center of projection. The perspectives of any two horizontal lines that are parallel to each other intersect the horizon line at the same point, which is their *horizontal vanishing point*.

Proposition 2. The perspectival images of parallel lines that are also parallel to the picture plane are parallel to each other; the perspectival images of parallel lines that are not parallel to the picture plane converge onto a vanishing point (which is not necessarily within the confines of the picture).

It can be confusing at first to realize that when one looks at a picture like Figure 1-9, one cannot tell whether the box was tilted and the picture plane was vertical, or the box was upright and the picture plane tilted (as we described it to be). Had we described it as the picture of a tilted box projected onto a vertical picture plane, then we would have had to relabel the vanishing points, for there would be neither horizontal nor vertical vanishing points and it would therefore be incorrect to label a line connecting two of the vanishing points "horizon."

This point can be further clarified by noting that in Figure 1-2 one projecting ray is singled out and given a name of its own: It is the *principal ray*, the projecting ray that is

27

perpendicular to the picture plane. (It is along this line that one measures the distance between the center of projection and the picture plane.)[6] In Figure 1-4, the principal ray intersects the picture plane at the horizon. This is true only in the special case when the picture plane is vertical. Nevertheless, although it is inappropriate to call a horizontal line drawn through the foot of the principal ray the "horizon," this line is meaningful and important. It is the locus of the vanishing points of lines orthogonal to the picture plane and parallel to each other.

We are now ready for the third property of perspective:

Proposition 3. The location of an object point cannot be determined uniquely by its image. However, it is possible, by making assumptions about properties of the scene, to solve the inverse problem of perspective, namely, given the central projection of a scene, to reconstruct its plan and elevation.[7]

For instance, Sanpaolesi (1962)[8] proposed the reconstruction of Masaccio's *Trinity* (Figure 1-1), shown in Figure 1-11.

To gain some insight into what Alberti taught his contemporaries, we should examine what Renaissance artists came to call the *construzione legittima* (legitimate construction) of the perspective drawing of a pavement consisting of square tiles. Figure 1-12 summarizes the geometry underlying the construction. To carry it out, one needs a plan (view from above) and an elevation (side view) of the pavement, on which are indicated the picture plane and the center of projection. In Figure 1-12, I have numbered

---

[6] Alberti (1966, p. 48) called the principal ray the "prince of rays."

[7] This problem was analyzed in great depth by Jules de la Gournerie (1814–83) in his monumental *Traité de Perspective Linéaire* (1884). Methods such as his have been applied to a fair number of works of Renaissance art. For a recent bibliography, see Welliver (1973).

[8] Although Janson (1967, p. 88, footnote 25) argues convincingly that Sanpaolesi's reconstruction contains errors, I have chosen to reproduce his rather than Janson's because its elevation shows the location of the figures, whereas Janson's shows only the architecture. (See also Battisti, 1971.)

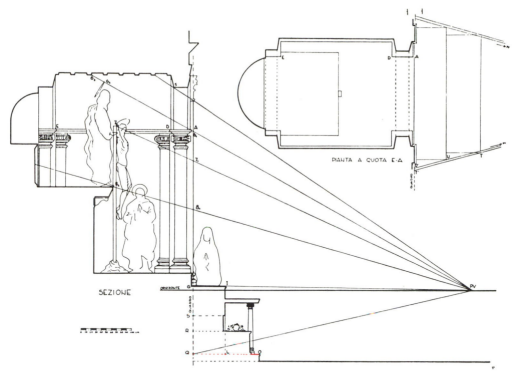

Figure 1-11. Plan and elevation of Masaccio's Trinity *according to Sanpaolesi (1962, figure C, opp. p. 52)*

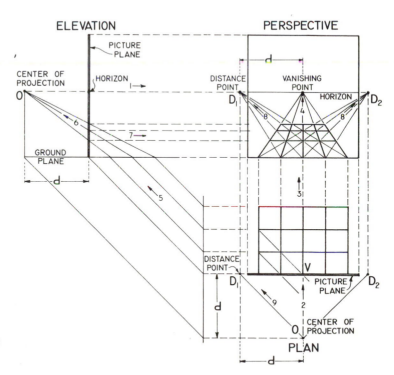

Figure 1-12. Construction of perspective representation of a pavement consisting of square tiles

29

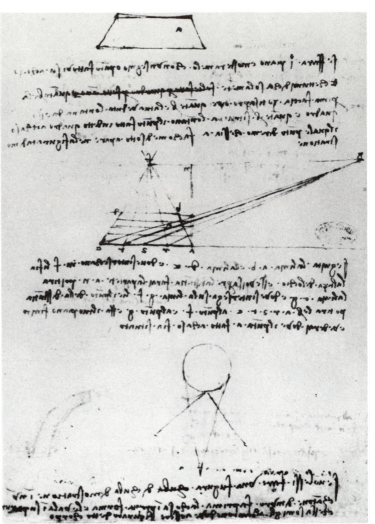

Figure 1-13. Leonardo da Vinci, Alberti's construzione legittima (ca. 1492). Manuscript A, Fol. 42ʳ. Bibliothèque de l'Institut, Paris.

the steps involved in constructing the perspective: (1) Use the elevation to draw the horizon. (2) Use the plan to determine the vanishing point on the horizon. (3) Use the plan to mark off the front of the pavement on the bottom of the picture. (4) Connect these points to the vanishing point. (5) Transfer the locations of the tiles from the plan to the elevation. (6) Connect these points to the center of projection in the elevation. (7) Transfer the intersections of these lines with the picture plane in the elevation. Figure 1-13 shows how Leonardo represented the procedure. Because the tiles in the pavement are square, Alberti (and Leonardo after him) was able to combine steps (3) and (5).

To verify the correctness of the construction, Alberti recommended that the artist draw the two sets of diagonals of the square tiles. Because each set consists only of parallel lines, each should converge to a vanishing point on the horizon; these are the *distance points* D_1 and D_2 in Figure 1-12. These distance points are important for a reason suggested by their name: In the *construzione legittima*, the distance between the vanishing point and each distance point is equal to the distance d between the center of projection and the picture plane.[9]

[To demonstrate this fact, find the central projection of a horizontal line, passing through the center of projection O and forming a 45-degree angle with the picture plane (line 9 in the plan of Figure 1-12). Because, as we have seen, all lines that pass through the center of projection are represented as a point, the representation of this line is the intersection of line 9 with the picture plane. This intersection is D_1, for line 9 is parallel to the diagonals that converge at that point. Now consider the triangle OVD_1. Because it is a right triangle with one 45-degree angle, it is isosceles; and because the length of OV is d, the length of D_1V is also d.   QED.]

[9] The distance points are known as a *conjugate pair* of vanishing points. For future reference, I wish to define this term: The perspective images of any two lines pass through their respective vanishing points. If the lines to be represented intersect, and if the angle of their intersection is a right angle, their respective vanishing points are said to form a *conjugate pair*.

31

Interlude: Brunelleschi's peepshow and the invention of perspective

The masters of the subtle schools
Are controversial, polymath.
> T. S. Eliot, from "Mr. Eliot's Sunday Morning
> Service," 1920 (Eliot, 1963, p. 58)

At least a decade before Alberti's theoretical work, Filippo di Ser Brunellesco (1377–1446) painted two panels in the course of an experiment that according to Edgerton "marked an event which ultimately was to change the modes, if not the course of Western history" (1975, p. 3; see also De Santillana, 1959).[1] Although these two panels have not been preserved, we know that they are the first paintings to correctly embody linear perspective. The first panel was a view of the church of San Giovanni di Firenze, later known as the Florentine Baptistery, as seen from a point about five feet inside the portal of the as yet unfinished cathedral of Florence, Santa Maria del Fiore, across the Piazza del Duomo. According to Brunelleschi's biographer of the 1480s, Antonio di Tuccio Manetti, in order to constrain the viewer to place his eye at the center of projection, Brunelleschi

had made a hole in the panel on which there was this painting; . . . which hole was as small as a lentil on the painting side of the panel, and on the back it opened pyramidally, like a woman's straw hat, to the size of a ducat or a little more. And he wished the eye to be placed at the back, where it was large, by whoever

---

[1] Gioseffi (1966) estimates Brunelleschi's first panel to have been done between 1401 and 1409; according to Kemp (1978), it is prior to 1413; Edgerton (1975) puts the date at 1425.

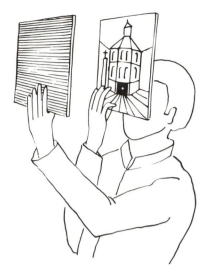

Figure 2-1. Edgerton's depiction of Brunelleschi's first experiment. Mirror was probably considerably smaller than panel, for optics require it to be only about half panel's size, and good mirrors were very difficult to make in the fifteenth century.

had it to see, with the one hand bringing it close to the eye, and with the other holding a mirror opposite, so that there the painting came to be reflected back; . . . which on being seen, . . . it seemed as if the real thing was seen: I have had the painting in my hand and have seen it many times in these days, so I can give testimony. (Trans. by White, 1968, pp. 114–17)

Figure 2-1 shows Edgerton's reconstruction of the first panel and how it was held. In Chapter 3, we will see that this method, Brunelleschi's peepshow,[2] is an effective method for the creation of an illusion of depth.

Manetti and Vasari thought that Brunelleschi had gone beyond this brilliant demonstration; they claimed he had invented perspective. Here is Manetti's account:

Thus in those days, he himself proposed and practised what painters today call perspective; for it is part of that science, which is in effect to put down well and within reason the diminutions and enlargements which appear to the eyes of men from things far away or close at hand: buildings, plains and mountains and countrysides of every kind and in every part, the figures and other objects, in that measurement which corresponds to that distance away which they show themselves to be: and from him is born the rule, which is the basis of all that has been done of that kind from that day to this. (Trans. by White, 1967, p. 113)

Manetti and Vasari notwithstanding, the current consensus is that he did not know the *contruzione legittima*.[3] It would take us too far afield to discuss the various ingenious reconstructions of the method Brunelleschi used in painting these panels without using the *construzione legittima*. But because there are some tantalizing clues to why his method did not become public knowledge, I would like nevertheless to explore the question of Brunelleschi's priority.

Mariano Taccola reported Brunelleschi to have said:

Do not share your inventions with many. Share them only with the few who understand and love the sciences. To describe too much of one's inventions and achievements is one and the same thing as to abase your talent. (Quoted in Kemp, 1978, p. 135)

---

[2] As Arnheim (1978) called it.
[3] Recent reconstructions of his methods are in Arnheim (1978), Edgerton (1975), Kemp (1978), Lynes (1980), and Pastore (1979).

Maybe he was loath to reveal his method, just as a magician is loath to disclose his gimmick.[4] According to Taccola, Brunelleschi had complained that

> many are ready, when listening to the inventor, to belittle and deny his achievements, so that he will no longer be heard in honourable places, but after some months or a year they use the inventor's words, in speech or writing or design. (From *De ingeneis*, see trans. by Prager and Scaglia, 1972, pp. 11-12).

Why would Brunnelleschi be afraid that people would belittle his achievements? Perhaps, as Lynes (1980) thinks, Brunelleschi had good reason to be secretive: He had used an empirical, not geometric, method to create his panels; but he deceived his contemporaries and claimed to be the originator of the *construzione legittima*. This is not inconsistent with Vasari's (1965) Adlerian analysis of Brunelleschi:

> There are many men whom nature has made small and insignificant, but who are so fiercely consumed by emotion and ambition that they know no peace unless they are grappling with difficult or indeed almost impossible tasks and achieving astonishing results. (p. 133)

In all fairness, we should note, however, that Vasari also wrote:

> Filippo was endowed with . . . such a kind nature that there was never anyone more gentle or lovable. . . . He never allowed his own advantage . . . to blind him to merit and worth in others. (pp. 133–4)

This encomium does little to mitigate the impression of Brunelleschi's ruthlessness left by Vasari's gripping description of his rivalry with Lorenzo Ghiberti over the assignment of the latter to share the commission to raise the cupola of Santa Maria del Fiore in Florence.

The story of this rivalry, as told by Vasari (1965), opens in 1417. Brunelleschi was among the several Florentine architects consulted on the difficult problem of raising the cupola. After Brunelleschi had worked out an approach to the problem,

---

[4] I will discuss this idea further in Chapter 8.

he took it into his head to return to Rome; . . . for Filippo thought that he would be valued more highly if he had to be sought after than if he stayed in Florence. . . . [The consuls and wardens] wrote to Filippo in Rome, begging him to return to Florence; and this being just what Filippo wanted, he very politely did what they asked. (p. 142)

After Filippo returned, he presented his ideas to the consuls and wardens and suggested that architects from Florence, Tuscany, Germany, and France also be consulted. Although his scheme was well-received, he was asked to make a model for the consuls to study. "However, he showed no inclination to provide one; and instead he took his leave of them, saying that he had been approached by letter to go back to Rome." The wardens begged him to stay, had his friends plead with him, offered him an allowance; but Filippo left for Rome. In 1420, Filippo and the foremost architects of his day were assembled to present their plans. Because Filippo's plan was by far the simplest, he was called "an ass and a babbler" and dismissed from the audience. But Filippo refused to leave and "he was carried out by the ushers, leaving all the people at the audience convinced that he was deranged." Nevertheless, Filippo managed to have another hearing called. At the meeting, he persisted in his refusal to present a model, but challenged

the other masters, both the foreigners and the Florentines, that whoever could make an egg stand on end on a flat piece of marble should build the cupola, since this would show how intelligent each man was. So an egg was procured and the artists in turn tried to make it stand on end; but they were all unsuccessful. Then Filippo was asked to do so, and taking the egg graciously he cracked its bottom on the marble and made it stay upright. The others complained that they could have done as much, and laughing at them Filippo retorted that they would also have known how to vault the cupola if they had seen his model or plans. And so they resolved that Filippo should be given the task of carrying out the work. (pp. 146–7)

But a group of workmen and citizens managed to persuade the consuls that Filippo should be given a partner. When Filippo heard that his friend Lorenzo Ghiberti, whom he

35

had assisted in polishing the superb reliefs Lorenzo had made for the doors of San Giovanni, had been selected as his partner and was to receive a salary equal to his own,

he made up his mind that he would find some way of insuring that Lorenzo would not last too long on the job. One morning or other [in 1426] Filippo . . . bandaged his head and took to his bed, and then, groaning all the time, he had everyone anxiously warming plates and cloths while he pretended to be suffering from colic. . . . After Filippo's illness had already lasted more than two days, the steward and many of the master-builders went to see him and kept asking him to tell them what they should do. But all he answered was: "You have Lorenzo; let him do something." (pp. 150, 152)

Seeing that the work on the cupola had almost come to a standstill, the wardens complained to Filippo, who said:

"Oh, isn't that fellow Lorenzo there? Can he do nothing? I'm astonished – and at you too!"
The wardens answered: "He will do nothing without you."
And then Filippo retorted: "I would do it well enough without him." (p. 153)

Filippo returned to work believing that he had persuaded the wardens to dismiss Lorenzo. But he was wrong; they didn't. And so "he thought of another way to disgrace him and to demonstrate how little knowledge he had of the profession" (p. 153). He proposed to the wardens in Lorenzo's presence that the next stage of the work be divided between them. Lorenzo was in no position to disagree and was allowed to choose the task he preferred. When Filippo had finished his part, Lorenzo had barely finished a fraction of his, and Filippo let it be known that Lorenzo's work was not competent. When the wardens caught wind of this, they asked him to show them what he would have done. Filippo's response impressed them so deeply that "the wardens and the other artists . . . realized what a mistake they had made in favouring Lorenzo." Filippo was made "overseer and superintendent for life of the entire building, stipulating that nothing was to be done save on his orders" (p. 155). Although Lorenzo was disgraced, he continued to draw his salary for three years, thanks to his powerful friends.

36

This episode is sufficient, I think, to undermine Vasari's depiction of Brunelleschi as a kind, gentle, and lovable genius who never was "blind to merit and worth in others." It is difficult to see him only as a victim, as Vasari concludes, "in some respects unfortunate" who "was always having to contend with someone or other." Even though Vasari testifies to Brunelleschi's good moral character, and claims that Brunelleschi only defended what was legitimately his against Lorenzo, there are nagging doubts: If Filippo had been Lorenzo's faithful friend, why did Lorenzo agree to share an honor he had not earned? And why was Brunelleschi so secretive? Did he really have a reason to fear plagiarism? After all, the other architects were willing to present their models and discuss their plans in public. Furthermore, we know that his secretiveness was not an attempt to hide incompetence; he was probably the only architect who knew how to raise the cupola of Santa Maria del Fiore.

But it may be that Brunelleschi's strange behavior in the episode of the cupola was the outcome of an attempt to hide the fact that his creativity was intuitive rather than analytic. Twice Brunelleschi did not give a theoretical account of a major achievement of his. Perhaps he knew how to erect the cupola but could not explain why this method was correct, just as he knew how to paint startlingly realistic and perspectivally correct panels without knowing the rules of the *construzione legittima*. When Brunelleschi invented perspective and when he sought the commission for the erection of the cupola, he may have been behaving as he had during the episode of the egg; that is, he may have invented a trick to paint pictures in perspective without having developed the underlying geometric theory, and he may have come up with methods to erect a tall cupola without having a rigorous rationale to offer. Perhaps in both cases he allowed people to infer that he understood the process more conceptually than he really did, and in both cases he was unreasonably worried about having allowed people to believe that he knew something that no one could legitimately expect him to know. As a result, he allowed people to think that he was mad rather than

37

present his plans for the cupola; perhaps for the same reason he destroyed the panels, in order to take his secret with him to the grave. Thus I believe that Alberti, and not Brunelleschi, invented perspective as a communicable set of practical procedures that can be used by artists. Otherwise Brunelleschi, driven by ambition as he was, would have made sure that Alberti did not receive acknowledgment of priority in the discovery of the *construzione legittima*. So Filippo was not only an extraordinarily ambitious, competitive, secretive, slightly paranoid, cunning, somewhat manipulative genius. He was, if my speculative analysis of his personality is correct, a man deeply concerned with disguising the nature of his creativity, afraid that he would not be held in high esteem unless he was thought to possess abstract theoretical knowledge.[5]

[5] I wish to thank Michael Sukale for suggesting that Brunelleschi may have only intuited the technique of raising the cupola without having formulated the underlying theory.

3 The effectiveness of Brunelleschi's peepshow

Brunelleschi's friends were amazed at the compelling impression of depth they experienced when they looked at his panel through the peephole in its back. How compelling could it have been? In this chapter, we will see that Brunelleschi had discovered an almost optimal technique to wrest an illusion of depth from a picture painted on a flat surface.

If one wishes to gauge the intensity of an experience of depth induced by a picture, it is best to compare it to the most effective technique available: the stereoscope. Figure 3-1 shows a stereoscopic pair of drawings prepared by Sir Charles Wheatstone in 1831 to demonstrate his discovery of the basis of stereoscopic vision to the Royal Society (Wheatstone, 1838). If you look at them as instructed in the caption, only one picture will be seen by each eye, and you will experience the full strength of the effect. To understand the effect, hold an object in your hand and look at it first with one eye and then with the other. Because each eye sees the object from a slightly different vantage point, the object casts a somewhat different image on the retina of each eye. Nevertheless, when both eyes are open we see only one object; we do not see double as we might naively expect. Of course, the visual system cannot fuse two images that are very different. To see how limited is our ability to fuse disparate images, hold up your two hands, side by side, a few inches apart, their backs facing your eyes, index fingers pointing up, about half a foot before your nose, and focus on one of your fingers. Make sure that you can see both fingers clearly. If you can't,

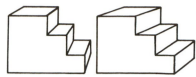

Figure 3-1. Wheatstone's stereoscopic drawing. Take a piece of thin cardboard (an index card will do) roughly 4 by 6 in. (10 by 15 cm). Place the book on a table, hold the card vertically between the two pictures (with its short dimension against the page), touch your nose to the card, and look at the right-hand drawing with your right eye and at the left-hand drawing with your left eye. Relax. The two drawings will appear to merge and you will see the object in depth.

move them closer to each other. Now slowly move the hand at which you were looking closer or further away. Over a short distance, both fingers will remain in focus, but after your hand has moved about an inch you will notice that the finger at rest looks double. This is because the visual system can only fuse the two disparate images that a single object casts on the two retinae if the so-called *retinal disparity* between these two images is not too large. The retinal disparity of the finger you were looking at remained zero while the retinal disparity of the other finger grew as you moved it away. Wheatstone demonstrated that if retinal disparity is small the two images not only fuse but also give rise to a most compelling experience of depth, called *stereopsis*.[1]

What is the function of stereoscopic vision? It gives us the ability to accurately gauge and compare distances in our immediate environment, approximately within range of a long jump, that is, a range of a few yards. For instance, you will find it extremely difficult – indeed almost impossible – to perform a task requiring fine perceptual–motor coordination at close range (such as threading a needle) with one eye closed.

There was a time when psychologists, impressed with the critical role played by stereoscopic vision in the performance of such perceptual–motor skills, thought that the world appeared flat when seen through one eye. The truth is that one-eyed people are not really handicapped at all when it comes to visual tasks that require them to aim action toward long-range targets, such as throwing a ball or landing an airplane. From this observation concerning our ability to effectively gauge depth with one eye, we might predict that a monocularly viewed picture that projects onto the retina the same image as might be projected by a three-dimensional scene would be seen in depth, because the picture would then be a *projective surrogate* for the scene. A projective surrogate was considered by Gibson

[1] The theory underlying stereoscopy was known to Leonardo. See Leonardo da Vinci, 1970, §534, p. 323.

40

(1954) to be a special case of the more general class of *surrogates*:

A surrogate will be defined as a stimulus produced by another individual which is relatively specific to some object, place, or event not at present affecting the sense organs of the perceiving individual. (pp. 5–6)

Surrogates fall into two classes: conventional and nonconventional. The nonconventional surrogates can also be subdivided:

Non-conventional, projective or replicative surrogates [are] characterized by . . . the theoretical possibility of the surrogate becoming more and more like the original until it is undistinguishable from it. (p. 11)

It is easy to create a projective surrogate: One draws a picture in rigorous perspective and places the observer's eye at the picture's center of projection. Unfortunately, the expectation that an exact projective surrogate would be seen in depth is not confirmed. Although we usually interpret such a picture as the representation of a three-dimensional scene when we view it from the appropriate vantage point, the impression is no more compellingly three-dimensional than if we viewed the picture from a different vantage point. The vividness of stereopsis is absent from this experience. Thus to view a rigorous perspective picture from its center of projection is not enough to transform our impression of a picture that represents depth into an experience almost indistinguishable from the perception of objects deployed in depth. At this point, we might conclude that only disparate images seen by the two eyes can produce the sort of vivid experience of depth we are discussing. Such a conclusion would be premature, as we shall presently see. Indeed, one might say that the reason we do not see vivid depth in pictures (whether viewed with one eye or two) is not because they fail to fulfill the necessary conditions for such perception, but rather because pictures bear two kinds of incompatible information, namely, information about the three-dimensional scene they represent, as well as information about their own two-dimensionality. It follows that if we could rid ourselves of

41

the latter, the former information should produce a vivid and compelling experience of depth, as striking as stereopsis.

One way to reduce the noticeability of the surface of a picture is to have the spectator view the picture from a long distance away. If the picture is so large as to enable the spectator to view the picture from afar, stereoscopic vision, which can under some conditions diminish the experience of depth by supplying us with information regarding the flatness of the picture plane, is ineffectual because of the distance. Indeed, it is unlikely that stereoscopic cues can tell us much about the flatness or the orientation of a picture that is more than 200 cm. (about 2 yd.) away from us (Ono and Comerford, 1977). So if the spectator's eyes are approximately at the center of projection of the picture and the picture plane is distant, we should perceive the picture in vivid depth. The typical work of art based on this principle is a wall or ceiling painting. It represents a scene in an architectural setting that, even though imaginary, is a continuation of the real architecture of the hall. The best example is Pozzo's ceiling fresco in the Church of Sant'Ignazio in Rome (Figure 3-2). The painting is a very precise central projection of an imaginary architecture onto the hemicylindrical ceiling of the church, which uses a center of projection at the eye level of a person standing on a yellow marble disc in the middle of the nave.[2] Maurice Henri Pirenne in his impor-

◄

Figure 3-2. Fra Andrea Pozzo, Saint Ignatius Being Received into Heaven *(1691–4). Fresco. Ceiling of the Church of Sant'Ignazio, Rome.*

[2] It is rather easy to dismiss this ceiling as kitsch, an example of the "enticing and popular iconography of sentimental baroque" that, according to Wylie Sypher (1978, p. 246), "accompanied a decay in rational theology and the rise of mere dogma in its place. The sensorium in its most literal activity became the instrument of faith. As the baroque imagination materialized itself at the familiar level, illusion became mere deception whenever the artist gave up the double world courageously erected by high-baroque art, and tried to obliterate entirely the distinction between the heavenly realm and the world of the worshipper. . . . Heaven is entirely accessible in Fra Andrea Pozzo's ceiling (1685 ff.) in Sant' Ignazio, where the majestic soaring architecture, itself painted, is almost obliterated by the swarming angelic hosts flying about the very windows of the clerestory and obscuring the values of both illusion and reality by their facile descent. This art makes transubstantiation 'easy' and credible."

43

tant book *Optics, Painting, and Photography* (1970) writes about Pozzo's ceiling:

The photograph, taken from the relevant yellow marble disc, shows the painting as it is meant to be seen. It shows little of the real architecture of the church, except the windows. To the spectator standing on the marble disc, the painted architecture appears *in three dimensions* as an extension of the real architecture. This photograph fails to give the overwhelming impression thus produced in the spectator by this vast painting. . . .

The result of all this work is striking . . . from the floor, the spectator is unable to see the painted surface, *qua* surface. It is impossible to determine where the ceiling surface actually is. From the position marked by the yellow marble disc, the arches supported by columns at both ends of the ceiling are seen to stand upright into space. They are seen in three dimensions, with a strength of illusion similar to that given by the stereoscope. . . . (Caption of Fig. 7.5, p. 81; p. 84)

The Pozzo ceiling is the culmination of a tradition of illusionistic painted architectures begun by Mantegna.[3] In the Ducal Palace in Mantua (Figure 3-3), he had painted an illusionistic parapet that appears to break through the ceiling. Around it, in extreme foreshortening, we see several *putti*[4] precariously perched on a narrow ledge and other figures peering down over the parapet. Almost half a century later, Peruzzi undertook a far more ambitious exercise in illusionistic imaginary architecture. On the walls of a room on the second floor of the Roman villa he designed for Agostino Chigi, the Pope's banker, he painted frescoes that represent balconies from which one can see beautiful views of Rome (Figure 3-4).

[Most of the published photographs of this wall fresco do not do justice to the power of the illusion it imparts, because they are not taken from the center of projection, which is not in the middle of the room, but in the doorway across the room from the right-hand door seen in Figure 3-4. For this reason, the imaginary architecture looks in these photographs as if it were askew with respect to the rest of the room. An exception is shown in Figure 3-5. See also Footnote 3, Chapter 4.]

---

[3] A survey of perspective paintings on nonvertical surfaces, which includes many of the works in this tradition, is Santapà (1968).

[4] Plural of *putto*, which is the Italian term for "cherub."

44

Figure 3-3. Andrea Mantegna, ceiling fresco (completed 1474). Camera degli Sposi, Palazzo Ducale, Mantua.

Neither of these works is extensive enough to provide an illusion as powerful as Pozzo's, nor did either artist prescribe an ideal vantage point from which the painting ought to be seen.

A second way to diminish the impact of cues for flatness was discovered about the middle of the seventeenth century when there flourished in the Netherlands a popular art – the "perspectyfkas," the perspective cabinet. Some of its practitioners were major artists of the Delft School, such as Pieter de Hooch and Jan Vermeer.[5] Pirenne describes one of them:

There is in the National Gallery in London a cabinet containing two peep-shows painted by S. van Hoogstraten (1627–1678). One of these peep-shows [reproduced in Mastai, 1975, plate 197] represents a seventeenth century Dutch interior consisting of a hall with a black and white tiled pavement, opening on two

[5] See Koslow (1967) for a review of perspective cabinets. Illustrations of all of them may be found in Leeman, Ellfers, and Schuyt (1976).

45

Figure 3-4. Baldassare Peruzzi, fresco (ca. 1515). Salla delle Prospettive, Villa Farnesina, Rome. Photograph taken from center of room (see Figure 2-5).

Figure 3-5. Peruzzi, fresco. Same as Figure 2-4, except that photograph was taken from center of projection of painting.

furnished rooms with a view of a street and a canal. All this appears in three dimensions when viewed through the peep-hole. This peep-show looks very much like a real interior, extending far beyond the dimensions of the cabinet. The scene is painted in perspective on the inside surface of the box, from one single centre of projection, the centre of the peep-hole. The painting is carried over in a continuous fashion from one wall of the box to another. In the hall the tiles, two chairs and a dog are painted partly on the wall, and partly on the floor of the box. It is hardly possible to tell on which surface of the cabinet the various parts are painted. When something of the actual wall of the cabinet can be distinguished, the painted view is seen 'through' the wall. (1970, p. 85, footnote 1; see also Wheelock, 1977)

46

Why is it "hardly possible to tell on which surface of the cabinet the various parts are painted"? Is it only due to the removal of stereoscopic cues to the disposition of the internal walls of the box? We should also consider the possibility that it is due to the peephole itself.

To understand peepholes, we must first deal with certain properties of lenses, which also apply to the lens of the eye. Consider a lens and a film (Figure 3-6). Consider also a field of object points (the gray region in panel A of Figure 3-6), the images of which are formed on the film by the lens. Even the best of lenses introduces some blur; in other words, the image of a point on an object is a circular region called the *circle of confusion*. The object points for which the circle of confusion is minimal are said to be in the *focus plane*. Object points that are less in focus than those in the focus plane, but are not objectionably blurred, are said to be *in focus* (panels B and C of Figure 3-6). The distance between the nearest object point that is in focus and the farthest object point that is in focus is called the *depth of field* of that lens.

Just as the distance of the focal plane of most camera lenses can be varied from infinity to a few feet, the visual system can change the shape of the eye's lens (a process called *accommodation*) and thereby vary the distance of the focal plane of the eye (over a greater range than most camera lenses). If an object is fairly close to the eye (say, less than 10 ft. away), the accommodation of the eye can be a source of information regarding the distance of the object; that is, the accommodation of the eye can serve as a range finder.

Cameras have diaphragms that make it possible to mask off part of the lens, to change the *aperture size*; similarly, the *iris* can change the size of the *pupil*. The smaller the aperture or pupil size, the less light hits the film or the retina. Changing the aperture size also affects depth of field. The smaller it is, the greater the depth of field (see Figure 3-6, panels D and E). Now if a peephole is so small that it effectively reduces the size of the pupil, it is called an *artificial pupil*. An artificial pupil can enhance pictorial depth by increasing depth of field and thus minimizing the

47

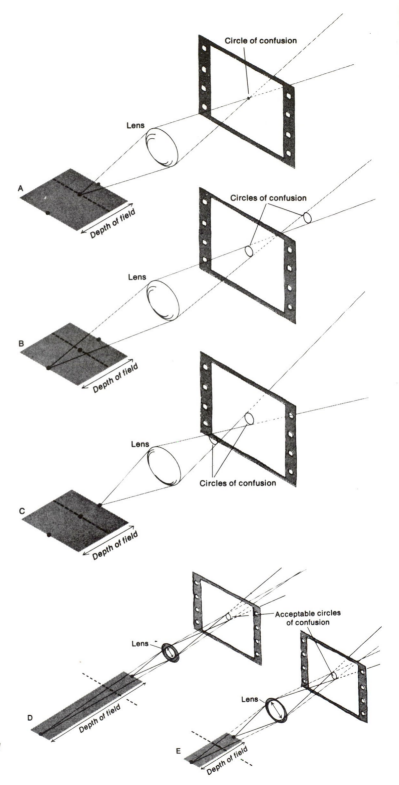

Figure 3-6. Focus and depth of field

value of information about distance derived from accommodation. For instance, when one looks into a relatively small perspective cabinet (as most are), the eye must focus on the painted surfaces inside the box; because the range is small, one might expect accommodation to disclose the distance of the painted surfaces and thereby diminish the illusion. This may be so, but if the peephole is very small, we should expect the viewer's depth of field to be increased. In such a case, the painting would be nicely in focus even if the eye accommodated so that its focus plane would be at the distance one might expect the walls of a real room to be.

In addition to affecting the depth of field, a peephole can also reduce information about the flatness of a painting just by truncating the visual field – by removing from sight the immediate foreground, surrounding objects, the picture's margin, and the unfocused (but possibly important) sight of one's nose (see Schlosberg, 1941, and Hagen and Jones, 1978).

So Brunelleschi's use of a peephole in his first demonstration was instrumental in producing a compelling experience of depth for two reasons: First, it increased the effectiveness of the illusion by forcing the viewer to place his or her eye at the center of projection of the perspective (thus making the picture a projective surrogate for the scene); second, it reduced the viewer's information regarding the flatness of the picture plane.

[The relative importance of these two factors is not known. For instance, we do not know the extent to which the apparent three-dimensionality of a display is diminished by the presence of stereoscopic cues to flatness. This question could be resolved by comparing the apparent three-dimensionality of a perspective painting seen monocularly through one peephole at the center of projection to the apparent three-dimensionality of the same painting seen binocularly through two peepholes on either side of the center of projection. An experiment by Adams (1972) compares these two conditions and includes a third: viewing through an artificial pupil. Although his data show no effect of the three modes of viewing, I do not consider the experiment definitive on this issue because of the method Adams used in determining perceived depth: He presented a picture representing a floor consisting of rectangular tiles, and a wall parallel to the picture plane that is the far wall of the room into

49

which the spectator is gazing. This wall was also divided into a row of tiles. The observers were asked to vary the height of the tiles on the far wall until they matched the depth of the floor tiles. Subjects systematically underestimated the depth of these foreshortened floor tiles by matching them to wall tiles that were always shorter in height than in breadth, whereas geometric considerations would predict the floor tiles to appear elongated in depth under certain conditions, square under other conditions, and elongated in width under a third set of conditions. This result could be accounted for by the subjects having performed a task that was a compromise between the task they were expected to perform, which required a judgment of depth (but may be difficult), and a comparison of the two-dimensional forms of the foreshortened tiles on the floor and the frontal tiles on the wall (which is likely to be easy). If the task that the subjects performed did not involve the judgment of depth to the extent anticipated, one cannot infer much about the different modes of viewing from the negative results reported.]

There is another aspect of Brunelleschi's technique that merits discussion. Although Brunelleschi's peepshow was similar to seventeenth-century perspective cabinets, it appears to have anticipated certain techniques for the enhancement of depth in monocularly viewed pictures that were not discovered until the first two decades of this century. Here is Harold Schlosberg's (1941) summary of these discoveries:

In the period around 1910, when interest in stereoscopy was high, it was widely known that the "plastic" effect could be obtained almost as well by viewing a single picture through a lens as by the use of disparate pictures in the binocular stereoscope. . . . The plastic depth that can be obtained monocularly is very striking, and must be seen to be appreciated. For optimal results the viewing lens should have the same focal length as the camera lens with which the picture was taken, but any ordinary reading glass works fairly well on pictures from 1-3 in. in size. In a typical snapshot of a person against a mixed background, the person stands out clearly, and plastic space can be seen between him and the background. In a good picture the person takes on solidity and roundness, with the slope of the lapel and the angle of the arms clearly in three dimensions. (p. 601)

For our purposes, it is most important to note that a similar effect can be achieved by "looking at a picture monocularly in a mirror. The mirror seems to break up the surface cues and may well have less obvious effects, such as destroying

50

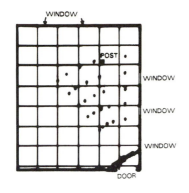

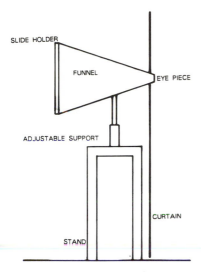

Figure 3-7. Experimental apparatus for Smith and Smith's experiment.

orientation" (Schlosberg, 1941, p. 603). This is exactly what Brunelleschi did.

In addition to all this nonexperimental evidence regarding the impact of Brunelleschi's peepshow, it has been shown in experiments that a proper central projection can be mistaken for a real scene if viewed monocularly from the center of projection. For instance, Smith and Smith (1961) asked subjects to throw a ball at a target in a room that they could view through a peephole (see Figure 3-7). Two groups of subjects threw the ball at a target in a real room. The subjects in one group were actually able to see the room through the peephole, whereas the subjects in the other group thought they were looking at the room but actually were looking at a photograph of the room. When subjects looked through the peephole at the real room, their throws were on the average quite accurate; when subjects looked through the peephole at a photograph of the room, the average throw was not systematically longer or shorter, but it was considerably more variable.[6] But what is more important than the similar accuracies of the throws was the absence of any awareness on the part of subjects that they had been seeing photographs in the viewing apparatus. In other words, neither in their performance of the ball-throwing task nor in their interpretation of the situation did the participants show any sign that the picture looked different from an actual room. And this implies that the Brunelleschi peephole can give rise to an illusion so strong that it could properly be called a delusion. We will return to this point in Chapter 5.

[6] The authors speculate that direct view of the targets permitted some monocular parallax and thus reduced the variability of the throws.

4 The robustness of perspective

Everywhere is here, once we have shattered
The iron-bound laws of contiguity.
> Robert Graves, from "Everywhere is here"
> (Graves, 1966, p. 431).

We have seen that Brunelleschi's peepshow, by placing the viewer's eye at the center of projection, can give rise to a compelling illusion of depth. Some students of perspective have thought that it can also protect the viewer from distortions one might expect to experience while viewing a picture from a point other than the center of projection. One of these was Leonardo:

> If you want to represent an object near you which is to have the effect of nature, it is impossible that your perspective should not look wrong, with every false relation and disagreement of proportion that can be imagined in a wretched work, unless the spectator, when he looks at it, has his eye at the very distance and height and direction where the eye or the point of sight [the center of projection] was placed in doing this perspective... otherwise do not trouble yourself about it, unless indeed you make your view at least twenty times as far off as the greatest width or height of the objects represented, and this will satisfy any spectator placed anywhere opposite to the picture. (Leonardo da Vinci, 1970, §544, pp. 325–6)

Why did Leonardo expect most paintings to "look wrong" when viewed from somewhere other than the center of projection? Because he was thinking about perspective in geometric terms. As we saw in Chapter 1, if it is known (or assumed) that a picture such as Masaccio's *Trinity* (Figure I-I) was generated according to the laws of central projection, it is possible, by making some assumptions about the scene, to reconstruct the scene.

Before a geometer can solve the inverse problem of perspective, the location of the center of projection must be determined. If an error is made in locating this center, the reconstructed scene will be distorted. For instance, in Figure 4-I, panel 97 is the inferred plan of the scene shown in panel 98 if the center of projection is assumed to be at point *o*. An observer standing at point *o* as specified in panel 97 would see a rectangular nave, as La Gournerie's plan shows. But if the center of projection is assumed to have moved to the left, as in panel 96, a geometer cannot solve the inverse perspective problem posed in panel 98 and still reconstruct a building whose ground plan is based on right angles. The ground plan in panel 96 is a *shear* transformation of the one in panel 97: Points of the plan in panel 97 are shifted laterally, parallel to the picture plane; the greater the distance of a point from the picture plane,

Figure 4-1. Drawings from La Gournerie, Traité de perspective linéaire. Panels 95, 96, and 97 represent plans of three geometrically correct solutions of inverse perspective problem posed in panel 98. In each of these solutions, ab is picture plane and o is center of projection.

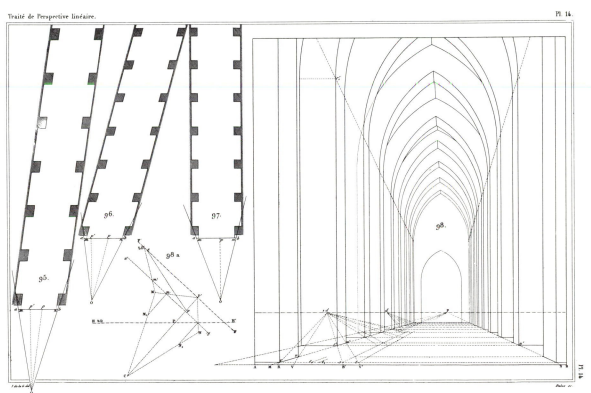

the greater the lateral displacement. (To visualize a shear transformation, imagine yourself holding a pack of cards and tapping the edge of the pack against the surface of a table, while the cards are at an oblique angle to the surface of the table.) If the assumed center of projection is moved laterally as much as in panel 96, but is also moved further from the picture plane, the shear transformation is combined with a *magnification*, as shown in panel 95. You may notice that the plan in panel 95 looks less distorted than does the one in panel 96. There are two reasons for this: First, the amount of shear is smaller in panel 95; p' is closer to p in panel 95 than in panel 96. Second, the greater the magnification, the smaller the angle at which the nave intersects the picture plane.

If perception solved the problem of inverse perspective in the same way as the geometer would, *and* if perception assumed that the center of projection always coincides with the perceiver's current point of view,[1] then an observer standing at point o as specified in panels 95 and 96 would see an oblique nave in accord with La Gournerie's plan.[2] As the reader can ascertain by moving in front of panel 98, no such striking distortions are experienced. I call this violation of our geometric expectations by our perceptual experience the *robustness of perspective*.

Such claims about the robustness of perspective have been made before, but not everyone agrees with the way the problem has been formulated and about the nature of the evidence in favor of robustness. For instance, Rosinski and Farber write:

Virtually every writer on pictorial distortion (the present ones included) has appealed to the reader's intuitions. For example, Haber (1978, p. 41) in discussing expected perceptions of dis-

---

[1] Assuming for the sake of simplicity that the perceiver's point of view is at a point.

[2] In recent years, several scholars have presented geometric analyses of the expected effects of viewing a perspective picture from a point other than the center of projection: Adams (1972), Farber and Rosinski (1978), Lumsden (1980), and Rosinski and Farber (1980). As far as I can tell, their only advantages over La Gournerie's analysis are their accessibility and their occasional pedagogical felicities.

torted pictorial space argues that "most picture lookers know that this does not happen." It is worth pointing out that neither such casual phenomenology nor the more experimental phenomenology of Pirenne is relevant here. The fact that observers are not consciously aware of distortions in virtual space [the depicted space] does not imply that the nature of virtual space is unregistered by the visual system. Furthermore, one's introspections about the nature of perceptual distortions are irrelevant. To comment on whether a picture seems distorted is to assess a correspondence between virtual space and the represented scene. A judgment of a distortion of space implies that virtual space is registered and somehow compared to environmental space. But, observers cannot judge that a scene is distorted unless they know what it is supposed to look like. This information is not available at the incorrect viewing point. Logically, one's estimate of the distortion present in virtual space can not be accurate unless an impossible object results. (1980, p. 150)

I vehemently disagree. The contrast between Leonardo's geometric expectations and our experience is the very issue at hand, the issue we wish to understand. No one has claimed that "the fact observers are not consciously aware of distortions in virtual space" implies "that the nature of virtual space is unregistered by the visual system." On the contrary, most theoreticians of picture perception (including Rosinski and Farber) believe that observers are not aware of distortions in virtual space because a part of the visual system (whose workings are unconscious) registers both the nature of the virtual space and the orientation of the surface of the picture, and corrects the former in the light of the latter.

Furthermore, Rosinski and Farber are wrong when they say that "to comment on whether a picture seems distorted is to assess the correspondence between virtual and environmental space." I think that to comment on whether a picture seems distorted entails a far richer implicit cognitive process: One must first mentally reconstruct the scene that the painter had in mind and then assess whether – within the conventions of the genre – the representation is correct. Take, for example, the exercise in perspective by the early seventeenth-century designer of architectural and ornamental pattern books Jan Vredeman de Vries (1968) shown

55

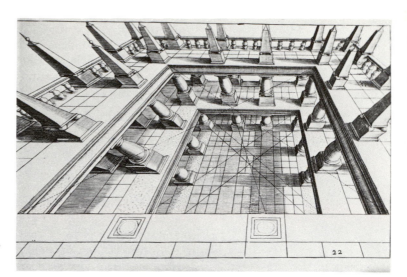

Figure 4-2. Jan Vredeman de Vries, architectural perspective

in Figure 4-2. Although technically in accord with the rules of central projection, the steles on the left are clearly distorted. We know this without ever having seen the architectural structures depicted and without being in a position to assess the correspondence between virtual and environmental space.

Returning to Leonardo's recommendation to artists, we can say that on the whole his worries were unfounded. In general, it is not necessary to view a picture from the center of projection to see an undistorted version of the scene it represents. Although it is true (as we will see later in this chapter) that certain types of objects seen under certain special points of view (such as eyes looking at the viewer, and the barrel of a gun or a finger pointing at the viewer) seem to follow us when we move in front of the picture, these are not the distortions Leonardo was worried about, and they are not true violations of the robustness of perspective.

And yet Leonardo was not entirely mistaken; there do exist conditions under which the geometer's expectations are confirmed and the robustness of perspective fails. We are fortunate to know about these conditions because they provide us with a clue to understanding what makes the robustness of perspective possible under most circumstances. The robustness of perspective fails when "the spectator is unable to see the painted surface, *qua* surface"

56

(Pirenne, 1970, p. 84); for example, in Pozzo's ceiling discussed in Chapter 3. Here is Pirenne's description:

> If the spectator walks away from the yellow disc, thus departing from the centre of projection, the illusion of depth does remain, but the scene represented, still seen in 3D, becomes deformed. The columns, for instance, look no longer vertical, and they may look curved. This deformation continually varies as one walks about in the church. The impression one gets is that the whole structure, which no longer appears in line with the actual church as an extension of it upwards, would be about to collapse if it were real.[3] (1970, pp. 84–5)

To prove Pirenne's thesis, one must show that (a) when the surface of a picture is hard to perceive, the virtual space of the picture is perceived in accordance with geometric expectations; and (b) when the surface of the picture can be seen, the virtual space of the picture is perceived to be invariant despite changes in the observer's vantage point.

Rosinski and his colleagues performed two experiments that provide exactly these sorts of data (Rosinski et al., 1980; see also Rosinski and Farber, 1980). Figure 4-3 shows how the stimuli were created. In panel 1, we see the object. Thirteen different photographs of this object were taken, as shown in panel 2; each was taken at a different angle of slant. In panel 3, we see one of these photographs appropriately cropped and mounted on flat black matte board. In Figure 4-4, we can see the apparatus used in the two experiments.

In the first experiment, Rosinski et al. simulated Brunelleschi's peepshow. They minimized the amount of information the observer would receive regarding the location of the picture plane by using a latter-day perspective-cab-

---

[3] Pozzo's ceiling differs from other paintings in two ways, either of which could in principle account for its greater propensity to distortion. First, there is Pirenne's theory: Only a painting whose surface can be seen *qua* surface manifests robustness of perspective. Second, most paintings are not designed to be seen as integral parts of architecture, so perhaps it is the discontinuity between the real and the virtual architecture for every vantage point other than the center of projection that is the cause of the distortion. I mentioned this point in discussing Peruzzi's *salla delle prospettive* in Chapter 3. It is important to conduct experiments to identify the relative contribution of these two causes.

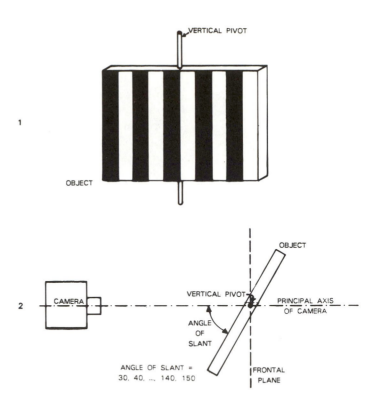

Figure 4-3. Preparation of stimuli in the Rosinski et al. (1980) experiments. (1) Frontal view of photographed object. (2) Top view of object, at 60-degree slant, and of camera. (3) Frontal view of perspective photograph of object at 60-degree slant.

inet with two peepholes: One peephole afforded a line of sight perpendicular to the surface of the photograph displayed in it; the other peephole shifted the observer's line of sight so that it formed a 45-degree angle with the surface of the photograph. To further reduce the visibility of the surface of the picture, Rosinski et al. put cross-polarized filters into the viewing box to minimize the amount of glare by diffusing the light reflected by the surface of the

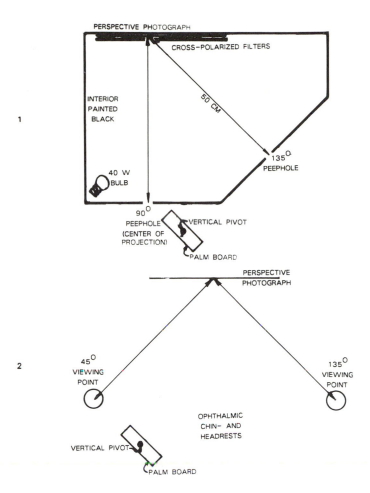

Figure 4-4. Presentation of stimuli in the Rosinski et al. (1980) experiments. (1) Experiment 1: Information regarding picture surface is minimized. (2) Experiment 2: Information regarding picture surface is not reduced.

photograph. The observer would be asked to view the photograph through a peephole at the center of projection, so that his or her line of sight would be orthogonal to the picture plane, or through a peephole from which the observer's line of sight would form a 45-degree angle with the picture plane (both were 50 cm or just under 20 in. from the picture plane). The observer's task was to adjust a palm board that could be rotated about a vertical pivot to indicate the perceived slant of the plane represented in the photograph.

In the second experiment, Rosinski et al. made no attempt to conceal the location of the picture plane, and therefore no viewing box was used: Observers were positioned 45 degrees to the right or 45 degrees to the left of

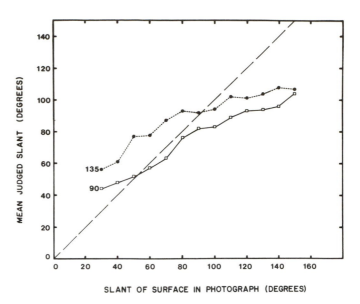

MEAN JUDGED SLANT (DEGREES)

SLANT OF SURFACE IN PHOTOGRAPH (DEGREES)

Figure 4-5. Data for Experiment 1 of Rosinski et al. Angle to which palm board was adjusted to match apparent slant of surface in photograph for the two points of view. Values of independent variable are determined by assumption that center of projection coincides with 90-degree point of view.

the center of projection, 50 cm away from the picture plane. The picture was viewed binocularly and the frame of the picture was visible.

Let us look at the results of the first experiment, shown in Figure 4-5. Look first at the line labeled "90." It presents the data for the adjustments made when the observers looked at the picture from the center of projection. Had the observers been able to correctly match the angle of the palm board to the slant of the surface in the photograph, the data points would fall on the dotted line. Because the data points deviate systematically from the line, we conclude either that subjects underestimated the extremity of the deviation of surface slants from the frontal plane or that they overestimated the extremity of the settings of the palm boards. The data do not allow us to decide which of these two interpretations is correct. Furthermore, the palm-board settings were invariably higher when the photographs were viewed from the oblique vantage point (labeled "135") than when they were viewed from the center of projection. This means that the photographs looked different when the observers viewed them from the two different vantage points, but not necessarily that the observers failed altogether to compensate for the change in vantage point. As we saw in Chapter 1, we can use ge-

60

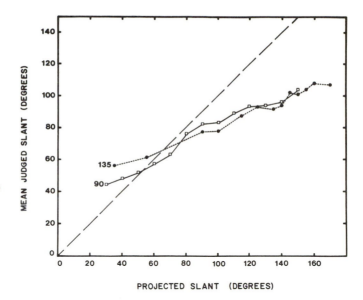

Figure 4-6. Modified data for Experiment 1 of Rosinski et al. Angle to which palm board was adjusted to match apparent slant of surface in photograph for the two points of view. Values of independent variable are determined by assumption that center of projection coincides with observer's point of view.

ometry to calculate what an observer who assumes that his or her eye is at the center of projection can legitimately infer about the represented scene. If we do that for the data shown in the curve for the eccentric point of view, the shape of that curve changes somewhat; on the whole, it shifts to the right and, as may be seen in Figure 4-6, appears to coincide with the curve for the data obtained for the view from the center of projection. In other words, the difference between the data obtained for the two vantage points is eliminated if one assumes that observers who viewed the picture through a peephole were unable to compensate for the change in vantage point, and that they perceived the photographs as if they assumed that the center of projection coincided with their vantage point.

Now we should turn to the results of the second experiment (shown in Figure 4-7). Here Rosinski et al. had made no attempt to reduce the perceptibility of the picture plane. The settings of the palm board appear to be no more accurate than in the first experiment; but the evidence regarding the robustness of perspective is unequivocal: There is no difference between the settings of the palm board for the two vantage points, thus demonstrating that the perceived slant of the plane represented in the photograph was independent of vantage point. So, Rosinski et al.'s exper-

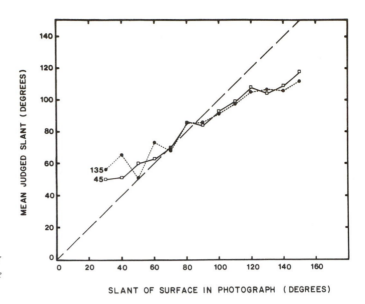

Figure 4-7. Data for Experiment 2 of Rosinski et al. Angle to which palm board was adjusted to match apparent slant of surface in photograph for the two points of view. Values of independent variable are determined by assumption that center of projection coincides with 90-degree point of view.

iment confirms Pirenne's hypothesis: If the subjects can see the picture plane, perspective is robust; if they cannot, perspective is not robust. In other words, the availability of information regarding the location and the orientation of the picture plane is necessary and sufficient for the robustness of perspective.[4]

Although in general perspective is robust, certain pictures are an interesting exception to robustness. I am referring to an illusion of "following" that we experience when we move in front of some paintings. Hans Wallach writes:

It is often noticed that the head of the portrait appears to turn when one walks past the picture. This apparent turning is even more impressive in the case of landscape that shows strong perspective depth. . . . I had noticed it first many years ago when walking past a landscape by Theodore Rousseau in the Frick Collection [see Figure 4-8]. It shows a country road flanked by rows of trees leading straight into the distance. When one walks past it, the whole scene appears to turn, the foreground moving with the observer. This rotation is the same as the portrait head's

---

[4] In Chapter 6, we will see that this conclusion is a bit too general. Information about the orientation of the picture plane is sufficient only if the picture is on *one* plane.

Figure 4-8. Pierre-Etienne-Théodore Rousseau, The Village of Bec-quigny (1857). The Frick Collection, New York. Subjects in Goldstein's (1979) experiment judged apparent orientations of road, rut in road, house, and line defined by the two trees in foreground.

which appears to turn as if to look after the passing viewer. (1976, p. 65)

This observation has been confirmed experimentally by E. Bruce Goldstein (1979), who affixed a black-and-white photograph of the painting by Theodore Rousseau mentioned by Wallach to an upright panel that could be turned right or left about a vertical axis. Rotating the panel was a convenient substitute for having the viewer walk around the reproduction. Just below the panel was a pointer that could turn independently of the panel about the same axis. The panel was shown to the viewer at several different viewing angles. For each angle, the observer was asked to adjust the pointer so that it would point in the same direction as the road. At all angles (ranging from 15 degrees, the right side of the painting turned toward the observer so that it was seen almost edge on, to 165 degrees, i.e., the left side of the painting turned toward the observer so that it was seen almost edge on), each observer set the

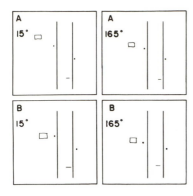

Figure 4-9. Schematic maps completed by two observers, A and B, at two viewing angles, 15 degrees and 165 degrees: To the two parallel lines representing road, they were asked to add a short line to represent rut in road, a rectangle to represent house, and two dots to represent trees.

pointer to point directly at him or her.[5] Because this result appears to run counter to the robustness of perspective, Goldstein performed a further experiment: The observers were shown the picture at various orientations and were given a schematic map with two parallel lines to represent the road. On this map, they were asked to mark the location of the closest house (on the left), of the two closest trees, and of a rut cutting across the road in the foreground. The maps (see Figure 4-9) were unaffected by the rotation of the picture, lending support to the robustness of perspective. I will explain the exceptions to the robustness of perspective in the latter part of the next chapter.

[5] When observers were asked to set the pointer to coincide with the orientation of other features of the scene, such as the line connecting the two trees on either side of the road in the foreground, the setting of the pointer varied systematically with the orientation of the picture. There is no explanation for this intriguing phenomenon.

5   Illusion, delusion, collusion, and perceptual paradox

Optical illusion
The twinkling of an eye, and the boxes on the floor
Hang from the ceiling. Really they are not boxes,
But only certain black lines on white paper,
(The programme of an hour of magic and illusion)
And, but for the eye, not even black on white,
But a vast molecular configuration,
A tremor in the void, discord in silence.
Boehme agrees with Jasper Maskelyne
That all is magic in the mind of man.

The boxes, then, depending on my mind
Hang in the air or stand on solid ground;
Real or ideal, still spaces to explore:
Eden itself was only a gestalt.

My house, my rooms, the landscape of my world
Hang, like this honeycomb, upon a thought,
And breeding-cells still hatch within my brain
Winged impulses,
(And still the bees will have it that the earth has flowers)
But the same dust is the garden and the desert.
Ambiguous nothingness seems all things and places.

Kathleen Raine (Raine, 1956, p. 93)

The pictorial effects we have been discussing all fall into the broad category of illusion. It is the purpose of this chapter to shed some light on the experience one can have when confronted with objects that fall under this rubric. The *Oxford English Dictionary* defines "illusion" as follows:

65

Figure 5-1. Stare at this square for about a minute in order to observe an afterimage. If you look at a distant wall after impressing afterimage on your retina, image will appear to be larger than if you look at a surface much closer to you.

Sensuous perception of an external object, involving a false belief or conception: strictly distinguished from *hallucination*, but in general use often made to include it, and hence equals the apparent perception of an external object when no such object is present, or of attributes of an object which do not exist. (1971 compact ed., s.v. "illusion")

One of the best-known examples of such a perception is called the *moon illusion*, the impression that the moon is larger when it is close to the horizon than when it is close to the zenith. Lloyd Kaufman and Irvin Rock confirmed in 1962 a theory that has been attributed to Ptolemy,[1] to wit, that the moon appears larger on the horizon than at the zenith because the filled space between the observer and the horizon makes the horizon seem further than the zenith[2] (Kaufman and Rock, 1962; Rock and Kaufman, 1962). There is an implicit inference here that is based on the following law: *All other things being equal, the further away an object (of constant angular subtense) seems to be, the larger it will appear to be.*

An especially pure example of the operation of this law was discovered by Emmert, in 1881. It is also easy to demonstrate. Look at the black square in Figure 5-1 for about a minute. When you look away, you will see a dark spot in front of you; this dark spot moves as you move your eyes, because it is caused by the neurochemical process by which the photosensitive cells in your retina recover from the unusually prolonged exposure that they sustained. Because this effect is impressed on the tissue of the retina itself, it must move with your eyes. At first blush, it may seem surprising that such a purely internal activity feels as if it were located outside you; but that is a general

[1] Claudius Ptolemaeus, a second-century astronomer and geographer who lived in Alexandria, author of the *Almagest*.
[2] The Kaufman-Rock theory has recently been challenged by Baird (1982), Baird and Wagner (1982), and Hershenson (1982). It is too early to determine the extent to which this new research will force a revision of Kaufman and Rock's theory. In any event, the purpose of the present discussion is to clarify the notion of unconscious inference and to set the stage for thinking about the nature of illusion. My argument does not hinge on the survival of any particular theory.

rule in perceptual systems: If one stimulates sensory receptors in a nonstandard fashion, one invariably experiences an external object that would stimulate the sensory receptors in a similar fashion. Now this sort of effect on the retina could just as well have been caused by a distant large square or by a close small one. Because an afterimage does not, so to speak, remember the distance of the page on which the stimulating square was printed, the size and distance of the black square that one experiences when having an afterimage would remain indeterminate were it not that perceptual systems abhor indeterminacy. (Try to think of what a square of indeterminate size and distance would look like.) To forestall such indeterminacy, the visual system uses the best available information about the size and the distance of the square: It assesses the distance of the surface at which the observer is currently looking, and, using that information and information about the size of the afterimage on the retina, it computes the size of the square to be seen. So if – after you have impressed an afterimage on the retina – you look at a distant wall, the square will look large; and if you look at a sheet of paper that is close to you, the square will look small. We can now state Emmert's law: *The apparent size of the object you see when you experience an afterimage is directly proportional to the perceived distance of the surface at which you are looking.*

The moon illusion and Emmert's law are both examples of an important way in which perceptual systems are endowed with the ability to perform what Helmholtz[3] called *unconscious inferences*, an idea that is central to what I wish to say about illusion and art in this chapter.[4]

Do we ever use the term "illusion" in the sense that applies to the moon illusion when we apply it to art? I think not: I do not think there *ever* is "false belief or conception" when we look at a work of art. Arthur C. Danto's discussion of illusion (in the sense of false belief or conception) shows clearly why we should hold this view:

---

[3] One of the great physicists and psychologists of the nineteenth century.

[4] For a contemporary presentation of the theory of unconscious inference, see Rock (1977 and, especially 1983).

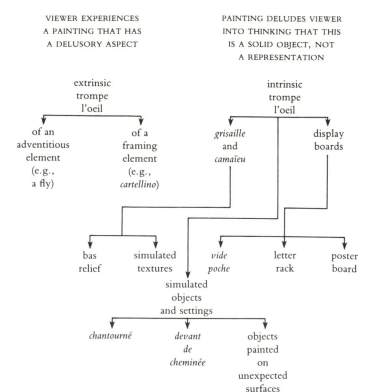

VIEWER EXPERIENCES
A PAINTING THAT HAS
A DELUSORY ASPECT

PAINTING DELUDES VIEWER
INTO THINKING THAT THIS
IS A SOLID OBJECT, NOT
A REPRESENTATION

extrinsic
trompe
l'oeil

intrinsic
trompe
l'oeil

of an
adventitious
element
(e.g.,
a fly)

of a
framing
element
(e.g.,
cartellino)

grisaille
and
camaïeu

display
boards

bas
relief

simulated
textures

vide
poche

letter
rack

poster
board

simulated
objects
and settings

chantourné

devant
de
cheminée

objects
painted
on
unexpected
surfaces

Figure 5-2. A classification of trompe l'oeil pictures

If illusion is to occur, the viewer cannot be conscious of any properties that really belong to the medium, for to the degree that we perceive that it is a medium, illusion is effectively aborted. So the medium must, as it were, be invisible, and this requirement is perfectly symbolized by the plate of glass which is presumed transparent, something we cannot see but only see through (as consciousness is transparent in the sense that we are not conscious of it but only of its objects) . . . So conceived, it is the aim of imitation to conceal from the viewer the fact that it is an imitation, which is conspicuously at odds with Aristotle's thought that the knowledge of imitation accounts for our pleasure. But imitation evidently did not entail illusion in Aristotle's scheme. In Plato's it evidently did, and it is this form of the theory I am working with now. Taken as a theory of art, what imitation theory amounts to is a reduction of the artwork to its content, everything else being supposedly invisible – or if visible, then an excrescence, to be overcome by further illusionistic technology. (1981, p. 151)

I take it for granted that the reader agrees with Danto's claim that the artwork should not be reduced to its content,

68

or else that he or she will read his persuasive argument in Chapter 6 of *The Transfiguration of the Commonplace*.

The only works of art that come close to exemplifying this sort of illusion are the illusionistic architectures we discussed in the preceding chapter and trompe l'oeil paintings. To better understand the role of illusion in art, let us examine this interesting aberration of art. I have classified the illusionistic paintings that go under the name *trompe l'oeil* (eye foolers) in Figure 5-2. The pictures fall into two major groups according to what the artist has represented.

A trompe l'oeil painting of the first kind *looks* like a painting; a delusory representation is superimposed on a painting that is taken by the viewer to be just that – a painting. I group these paintings under the rubric of *extrinsic* trompe l'oeil. There are two subgroups in this class. First, there are paintings in which an element foreign to the painting is painted to *look* like a foreign element. For instance, Carlo Crivelli's *Saints Catherine of Alexandria and Mary Magdalene* (see Figure 5-3), shows a fly on the left side of the left-hand niche.[5] We may say that such paintings are trompe l'oeil of an *adventitious element* (e.g., the fly). The second sort of extrinsic trompe l'oeil is a play on the viewer's expectations regarding the frame or framing elements.[6] For example, Antonello da Messina, in his *Salvatore Mundi* (Figure 5-4), painted a *cartellino* (little card), a trompe l'oeil representation of a creased piece of parchment bearing an inscription. As Marie-Louise d'Otrange Mastai (1975) has pointed out, Antonello's use of the *cartellino* is in keeping with the earlier device used by portrait painters: Sometimes they would paint an incised inscription on the parapet or sill in the foreground that creates the impression that the subject of the portrait is very close to the picture plane. An example is Jan van Eyck's *Portrait of a Young Man* (Figure 5-5). Eventually, when the parapet

[5] Two other examples of trompe l'oeil flies: *Portrait of the Artist and His Wife* by the Master of Frankfurt, and *Madonna and Child* by Adriaen Isenbrandt in the Akademie der bildended Künste, Vienna (see Mastai, 1975, p. 87).

[6] On the cognitive psychology of explicit and implicit frames that provide structure to our experience in society, see Goffman (1974).

was abandoned, whenever the *cartellino* was retained, it
became more thoroughly trompe l'oeil by appearing to be
pasted on the surface of the painting itself. One such case
is Francisco de Zurbarán's *Saint Francis* (Figure 5-6). Another use of framing elements for the purposes of trompe
l'oeil is the representation of a broken glass in front of the
painting. An example is a painting by Laurent Dabos (Figure 5-7).

The second class of trompe l'oeil paintings, if successful,
are not read as paintings at all. I consider them instances
of *intrinsic* trompe l'oeil. They fall into three categories: (1)

70

Figure 5-4. Antonello da Messina, Salvatore Mundi (1465). The National Gallery, London.

simulated texture or relief, (2) simulated objects or settings, and (3) display boards.

To simulate a bas relief or a texture, one needs for the most part to work in monochrome. When gray stone is to be simulated, the technique is called *grisaille* (the term comes from *gris*, the French for gray). If the material is not gray – such as bronze, terra-cotta, onyx, marble, or wood – a trompe l'oeil painting that simulates any of them is called *camaïeu*.[7] Figure 5-8 shows an example of this technique.

[7] This French word once was synonymous with cameo, but its meaning became restricted in the early eighteenth century.

71

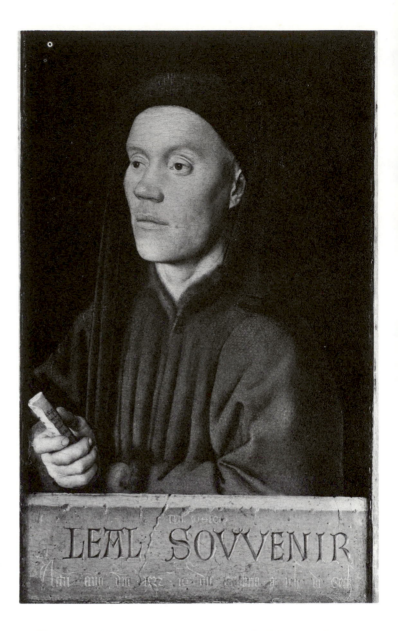

Figure 5-5. Jan van Eyck, Portrait of a Young Man *(1432). The National Gallery, London.*

There are three sorts of trompe l'oeil objects and settings: (a) cutouts, (b) hearth screens, and (c) objects painted on odd surfaces. *Chantourné* (literally, cutout), is a trompe l'oeil representation designed to stand away from a wall. An example is Cornelis Gijsbrechts's *Easel* (Figure 5-9).[8]

---

[8] See also Antonio Forbora, *The Artist's Easel* (1686), Musée Calvert, Avignon.

72

Figure 5-6. Francisco de Zurbarán, Saint Francis in Meditation *(1639). The National Gallery, London.*

The effectiveness of *chantourné* paintings relies on an impression of solidity derived from the shadows they cast on the walls behind them. Often, as in the case of *Easel* the *chantourné* includes a painting, usually a skillfully illusionistic one. The hearth screen, *devant de cheminée*, a French invention, was quite popular during the late seventeenth and the eighteenth centuries. This type of painting fools the eye because we do not expect a screen there, and whatever is represented is mundane and does not violate our expectations regarding what we might find in an unused hearth during the summer. The objects are strongly illuminated in the foreground and quite dim in the background, where the niche of the hearth casts a shadow. Even Jean-Baptiste Chardin painted one (Figure 5-10). If the hearth screen is designed to disguise the existence of the surface on which it is painted, there is a similar trompe l'oeil effect that can be obtained by painting on a surface

73

Figure 5-7. Laurent Dabos, Peace Treaty between France and Spain *(after 1801). Musée Marmottan, Paris.*

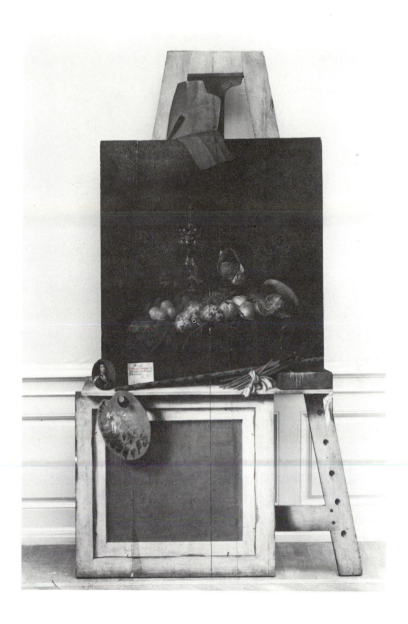

*Figure 5-9. Cornelis Gijsbrechts,
Easel (1633). Statens Museum for
Kunst, Copenhagen.*

◄

*Figure 5-8. French School, Rome
(early nineteenth century). Cooper-
Hewitt Museum, New York.*

that is an unlikely candidate to play such a role. An example
is van der Vaart's *Painted Violin* (Figure 5-11).

We finally come to the best-known class of trompe l'oeil
paintings – the several types of display boards. For example: Figure 5-12, the hunting trophy; Figure 5-13, the
quod libet (what you will), which eventually evolves into
the letter-rack; Figure 5-14, the *vide poche* (pocket emptier);
and Figure 5-15, the poster board.

Figure 5-10. Jean-Baptiste Chardin, The White Tablecloth *(1737)*. *Shows* devant de cheminée. *The Art Institute of Chicago.*

Figure 5-11. J. van der Vaart (at-trib.), Painted Violin *(late seventeenth or early eighteenth century)*. *Devonshire Collection, Chatsworth, England.*

Although it would take us too far afield to engage in an analysis of the significance and psychological bases of these trompe l'oeil works, I do want to point out the role of attention and expectation in creating the delusions to which these works can give rise. John Kennedy has taken a first step toward elucidating the role of attention in trompe l'oeil phenomena. He asked children to add a drawing of a figure in the midst of the children shown in Figure 5-16. When they concentrated on the central region of the picture, many of them absentmindedly tried to pick up the pencil. This observation suggests that although the standard claim about trompe l'oeil – namely that it requires the representation of an object of shallow depth – is true enough, it fails to do justice to the psychological complexity of the phenomenon. It is perhaps correct as a statement of a necessary condition for the occurrence of the trompe l'oeil effect, but it leaves the question of the effect's sufficient conditions unasked.[9]

[9] See Liotard (1973, Chapter 1), cited in Gombrich (1969, p. 430). See also interesting discussions in Gombrich (1969, p. 430) and a major historical review in Mastai (1975), upon which the above discussion leans heavily. There are also briefer reviews in Dars (1979) and Leeman, Elfers, and Schuyt (1976).

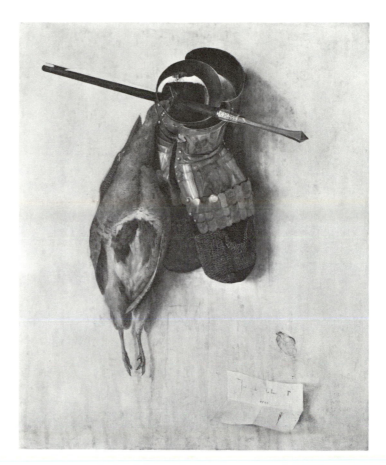

Figure 5-12. Jacopo de'Barbari, Dead Partridge *(1504). Alte Pi-nakothek, Munich.*

What is it about the delusion of trompe l'oeil that makes such works interesting? After all, there is nothing fascinating in a trompe l'oeil painting until the delusion has been dispelled; and once it has been dispelled, the work is most often of no more than minor esthetic interest. We enjoy examining an object endowed with the power to throw us into a delusory state of mind after it has divulged its secret to us; looking at it sends a shiver down our metaphysical spines much in the way we shiver when we think about an accident in which we were almost involved; we stare at it much as we might stare at the carcass of a wild animal that almost got the better of us. A trompe l'oeil picture is an epistemological close call, a reminder that Descartes's evil being that continuously fills us with error may be disguised as a benevolent painter. The point I wish to make therefore is that what is interesting about

77

Figure 5-13. Edward Collier,
Quod Libet *(1701). Victoria and*
Albert Museum, London.

a trompe l'oeil painting arises in our minds after the painting has ceased to *trompe* our *yeux*; it is when we have ceased to be the unwitting targets of a practical joke, and we have decided to reflect upon the experience we have just gone through, that the painting acquires its meaning.

And then looking at a trompe l'oeil painting after the delusion has been dispelled is fascinating because it shows us how utterly preposterous was Ruskin's famous idea of the "innocent eye." One tries in vain to be deluded again, but one can't; at best we are impressed by an illusion, which we obtain by actively cooperating with the artifices devised by the artist. But there is always a sense of innocence lost, a banishment from paradise, a fool's paradise to be sure, but paradise nevertheless.

All illusionistic art other than trompe l'oeil relies for its effect on a collusion between the artist and the spectator.

78

Consider illusionistic paintings of architecture for a moment. None of these paintings places the spectator at the center of projection at the moment the picture becomes visible. For instance, Pozzo's imaginary architecture in the Church of Sant'Ignazio looks lopsided unless it is seen from the yellow marble disk in the center of the church's nave: Therefore, only a visitor who would have asked to be led blindfolded to the prescribed vantage point would see the painting correctly, as it were, at first sight; but to have prepared one's experience so carefully presupposes prior knowledge of the spectacle one was about to behold and enjoy. Most viewers deeply enjoy the experience despite having first seen it lopsided and distorted. These viewers

Figure 5-14. Samuel van Hoogstraten, Still Life *(1655). Gemäldegalerie der Akademie der bildended Künste, Vienna.*

79

Figure 5-15. Wallerant Vaillant, Four Sides (mid-seventeenth century). Galleria Lorenzelli, Bergamo, Italy.

are in mental collusion with the artist who designed and painted the illusionistic architecture because they know full well that they are experiencing an illusion when they view the ceiling from the center of projection.

This concept of mental collusion is similar to Coleridge's "willing suspension of disbelief for the moment, which constitutes poetic faith" (1907, Book II, Chapter 14, p. 6). The difference is one of degree: Willing suspension of disbelief refers to a cognitive operation, a voluntary adoption of a certain aesthetic attitude; by mental collusion with the artist, I mean an operation much closer to the roots of perception, more on the order of a suggestion than a frame of mind.

The concept of mental collusion appears in nonaesthetic perceptual contexts as well. For instance, certain illusions do not occur spontaneously or involuntarily; they occur

Figure 5-16. Drawing used by Kennedy

Figure 5-17. The vase–face reversible figure.

only after the viewer is informed what he or she is expected to see. But once that knowledge is imparted, there is little the viewer can do to escape its effect. As an example, consider the experiment in which Girgus, Rock, and Egatz (1977) measured the time it took observers to experience a figure–ground reversal in Rubin's (1915) vase–face figure (see Figure 5-17), which was thought to spontaneously reverse back and forth between the vase percept and the face percept. The observers were high-school students who had never seen the Rubin figure before. Every 5 seconds, the experimenter tapped a pencil to mark the moment at which the observer was to report what he or she was seeing in the figure. Every effort was made to communicate to the observers that certain figures could be described in more than one way, and that therefore their reports could differ from signal to signal, but they were not told that the Rubin figure was reversible and they were not told what the alternative descriptions could be. After having obtained the observers' reports, the experimenter interviewed them to ascertain whether unreported reversals had occurred at every tap. Even with this scoring procedure, which was most likely to overestimate the number of reversals seen spontaneously, only 50 percent of the observers saw the figure reverse within the first minute of viewing, a figure that went up to 60 percent within the first two minutes and to 65 percent within the first three minutes. During the interview, observers were taught to see both alternatives and to grasp the reversibility of the figure. Afterward, the observers were tested again and, as expected, all of them reported reversals.

To better clarify the notion of mental collusion, let us look at the wonderful illusion invented by Bradley, Dumais, and Petry (1976; see Figure 5-18). The initial impression one receives is of a white paper cutout of a Necker cube superimposed on a sheet of white paper on which eight black disks have been drawn in order to enable you to see the figure's critical features. Even though there are no lines joining the corners, you see them, an unconscious inference regarding the nature of the object that would create this sort of configuration. You are not free to see

81

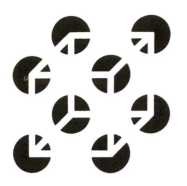

Figure 5-18. A Necker cube formed by cognitive contours as a perceptual analog of willing suspension of disbelief

or not to see these cognitive contours: If you see the Necker cube as I described it, you always see the contours. When you do, you also can see the cutout as a representation of a three-dimensional object, and, because the representation is ambiguous, you can see it reverse, as does the Necker cube. Now the interesting twist to this illusion comes when one's attention is drawn to another way of interpreting the eight spots. Imagine a sheet of paper with eight holes in it, and under it a sheet of black paper that can be seen through the holes. Now suppose we took the white paper cutout of the Necker cube and slipped it between these two sheets so that the critical features were visible through the eight portholes in the top white sheet of paper. When you interpret the figure in this fashion, you can still "see" the Necker cube, and you can still experience reversals of its orientation, but *you do not see the cognitive contours.* The act of choosing to see the cutout of the cube behind a page with holes in it rather than in front of the page with spots on it is very much like a willing suspension of disbelief. But once one has made a commitment to that suspension of disbelief, the world we perceive is consistent with how we have chosen to perceive it. It is important to remember that we are not in a position to reinterpret every facet of our perceptual experience and to see how the implications of our choice propagate through the remainder of our experience. But there are certain aspects of experience that allow us to make such a choice, although, unfortunately, we do not understand what gives them this power.[10]

[10] It is interesting to think of the complexity of representation and to speculate on how many levels of representation can be embedded in each other. The simplest case I know is the drawing on a cereal box of a boy holding a cereal box, on which there is a drawing of a boy holding a cereal box, on which . . . This case is easy, because we need not keep track of which representation is represented by which. All we have to do is invoke a perceptual "etc. experience," well-described in Gombrich (1969, pp. 219–21). In language, the limit is memory: We are hard put to unravel the sentence, "The mouse that the cat that the fire burned ate." Any more deeply embedded phrases would render the sentence incomprehensible without resorting to syntactic analysis. In the case of Bradley, Dumais, and Petry's illusion, we have two levels: a drawing of a cutout and its background (one level of representation), and the cutout representing a cube (an embedded representation).

We appreciate illusionistic art without being deluded; we know that what we are seeing is mere artifice; we experience illusion because we are in collusion with the artist. In contrast to illusionistic art, we appreciate trompe l'oeil because we were initially deluded. Mental collusion has very little to do with our appreciation of these creations, which, if we appreciate them at all, are reminders of the fallibility of knowledge acquired through the senses.

Having discussed the nature of delusion in trompe l'oeil and the nature of collusion in illusionism, we turn now to a third anomalous state of mind we sometimes experience when viewing a painting, namely, perceptual paradox. In the preceding chapter, we discussed the sorts of deformations we perceive in paintings *despite* the fact that in general perspective is robust. Although it seems paradoxical that, at one and the same time as one passes in front of a painting, the scene appears to turn and to remain the same, it is possible because not all aspects of our perception are processed by the same mechanisms; there is a division of labor that usually works so well that it is not noticed. The well-trained bureaucracy of the mind can deal with practically all the contingencies that occur in our environment. But when psychologists contrive devices that stimulate us in unusual ways, ways that are unlikely to arise in our environment, perception can be made to reveal the division of labor without which it could not function. The rules by which the bureaucracy has been accustomed to work may now lead to incompatible decisions.

For instance, take the *waterfall illusion*: On a screen, we display an unbroken series of horizontal black stripes moving downward. After a viewer stares at this stylized waterfall for a while, the motion is stopped, and he or she is asked to report what the display looks like. The display looks paradoxical: The stripes appear to be moving upward, but at the same time each stripe does not seem to be changing its position relative to the frame of the screen. This sort of perceptual decomposition has led to the hypothesis, now well-supported by experimental evidence, that motion and location in space are processed by different mechanisms (Attneave, 1974). No less interesting, though,

Figure 5-19. The vertical–horizontal illusion

is the following implication of the phenomenon: The visual system makes no attempt to reconcile these contradictory pieces of information about the world; we experience these unreconciled contradictories, this perceptual paradox, as *illusion*.

It is important to keep in mind the distinction between illusion as perceptual error, which we have called delusion, and illusion as an *awareness* of perceptual error, which we have called collusion. As we have seen in our discussion of the vase–face illusion, most illusions do not provide us with the experience of illusion unless we are given an opportunity for collusion, an understanding of what we are to expect to experience. Take, for instance, the vertical–horizontal illusion (Figure 5-19). The vertical looks longer than the horizontal: That is a perceptual error. But it is only when you are put in a position to experience a perceptual dilemma – such as being told to rotate the drawing slowly, and becoming aware of the changes in the relative lengths of the two lines during the rotation, while realizing that the drawing itself is invariant – that you may experience an illusion. This is a *metaperceptual experience*: It is an awareness of perceptions; the visual system does not try to reconcile the two experiences, and that nonreconciliation gives rise to the experience of illusion.

The impression of following in a painting is one of those rare instances where an object *spontaneously* gives rise to the experience of an illusion. My explanation of this phenomenon is schematically summarized in Figure 5-20. The experience of the picture turning stems from two perceptions: On the one hand, even though we are walking around the picture, we perceive the spatial layout of the represented scene as if it remains unchanged. This is what we have called in Chapter 4 the robustness of perspective (which we will discuss at length later). On the other hand, even though the spatial layout of the scene remains unchanged, we perceive our own motion in space as we walk past the picture. The experience of rotation of the painting is one way to resolve this dilemma: To perceive the scene as being invariant while we are walking past it, we must perceive the picture to be rotating.

84

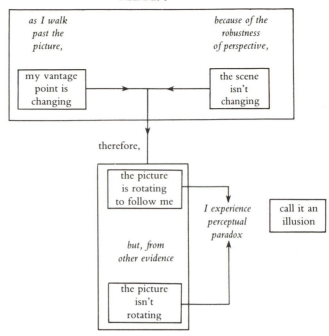

as I walk
past the
picture,

because of the
robustness
of perspective,

my vantage
point is
changing

the scene
isn't
changing

therefore,

the picture
is rotating
to follow me

I experience
perceptual
paradox

call it an
illusion

but, from
other evidence

the picture
isn't
rotating

DILEMMA 2

Figure 5-20. The double dilemma of picture perception that leads to the experience that the turning of the picture, as we walk past it, is illusory

As Gombrich has pointed out,[11] this resolution of the dilemma is reinforced in paintings that contain objects with a pronounced aspect such as a foreshortened gunbarrel, a pointing finger, a human eye, or a road receding into the distance from the center foreground to the horizon (such as the Rousseau painting discussed toward the end of the preceding chapter). These are objects that are represented in an orientation that is *visually unstable*: If you are looking down the barrel of a gun, you need to take only a very small step sideways in order not to be looking down the barrel of the gun. We say here that objects are represented in a visually unstable orientation by analogy with objects that are in a physically unstable equilibrium, such as a pyramid that has been balanced on its tip: You need to apply only a minuscule change to the forces exerted upon

[11] See Gombrich's essay, "Perception and the Visual Deadlock," in Gombrich (1963); also see Gombrich (1973).

85

the pyramid to cause it to fall.[12] It is quite natural, therefore, that we perform the unconscious inference: The object is shown in a visually unstable orientation; I am moving enough to destabilize the view; the view is not destabilized; therefore, the object must be turning to follow me.

But that solution to the dilemma is, so to speak, short-sighted, because it gives rise to another dilemma: If the picture is turning, how is it that it looks so well attached to the wall? Why does its relation to the room not change? The experience of illusion stems from the visual system's inability to resolve this dilemma within a dilemma.

Although we have shown that some distortions do take place in the perception of paintings that are viewed by moving observers, it is the robustness of perspective that emerges most clearly from our analysis. As we will see presently, it is this robustness that is probably the most important justification for not using Brunelleschi peep-holes to view perspective paintings.

[12] This formulation is inspired by Shepard (1981, pp. 307–9), who refers to René Thom's (1975) *catastrophe theory*. A similar notion can be found in the work of Huffman (1971), who calls *accidentals* what we have called "visually unstable orientations." See also Draper (1980). Anstis, Mayhew, and Morley (1969) have shown that the position of the iris and pupil with respect to the eye socket and the eyelids is sufficient to determine the perceived direction of a gaze. If the iris and the pupil are centered, we feel that the person is looking directly at us. Hence, if we move and the gaze remains directed at us, we perceive the gaze to be following us.

6 Perceiving the window in order to see the world

The picture is both a scene and a surface, and the scene is paradoxically seen behind *the surface. This duality of information is the reason the observer is never quite sure how to answer the question, "What do you see?" For he can perfectly well answer that he sees a wall or a piece of paper.*

J. J. Gibson, from *The Ecological Approach to Visual Perception* (Gibson, 1979, p. 281)

We have seen (in Chapter 4) that pictures drawn in perspective suffer very little distortion when they are not seen from the center of projection. Even though the Renaissance artists did not write about the robustness of perspective, they must have understood that paintings can look undistorted from many vantage points. In fact, soon after the introduction of linear perspective they began to experiment most audaciously with the robustness of perspective. As John White points out, Donatello's relief *The Dance of Salome* (or *The Feast of Herod*), shown in Figure 6-1, in the Siena Baptistery, "is less than two feet from the top step leading to the font, and well below eye level even when seen from the baptistery floor itself" (White, 1967, p. 192).[1]

In this chapter, we will explore the underpinnings of the robustness of perspective, and we will see why the phenomenon does not occur unless the surface of the picture

---

[1] Chapter 13 of White's book discusses several other frescoes and reliefs that have an inaccessible center of projection. No one has done the inventory of Renaissance art with respect to this phenomenon. We will return to the question of inaccessible centers of projection in the next chapter.

87

Figure 6-1. Donatello, The Feast of Herod *(ca. 1425). Gilded bronze panel, baptismal font, Cathedral of San Giovanni, Siena.*

is perceptible. In other words, we will discover that the Alberti window differs from all others in that it functions properly only if it is not completely transparent: We must perceive the window in order to see the world.

Look back at Figure 4-1 and imagine a geometer familiar with Gothic arcades who has been asked to solve the inverse perspective problem given that *o* as depicted in panel 95 is the most likely center of projection. Our geometer can now do one of two things: accept the suggested center of projection, in which case the solution will be a plan very much like the one shown in panel 95, a plan such as no Gothic architect would envisage in his most apocalyptic nightmares, or assume that the arcade is in keeping with all other Gothic architecture, with respectable right angles and columns endowed with a rectangular cross section, such as is shown in panel 97. The latter assumption implies that the center of projection of the picture does not coincide with the one suggested. Thus the observer is faced with a dilemma: to ignore the rules of architecture, or abandon the suggested center of projection and choose one in keeping with the rules of architecture. This is the geometer's *dilemma of perspective*, which the visual system too must resolve.

The robustness of perspective shows that the visual system does not assume that the center of projection coincides with the viewer's vantage point. For if it did, every time the viewer moved, the perceived scene would have to change and perspective would not be robust. Indeed, the robustness of perspective suggests that the visual system infers the correct location of the center of projection. For if it did not, the perceived scene would not contain right angles where familiar objects do. We do not know how the visual system does this. I will assume that it uses methods similar to those a geometer might use. Such methods require two hypotheses: (1) the *hypothesis of rectangularity*, that is, to assume that such and such a pair of lines in the picture represents lines that are perpendicular to each other in the scene, and (2) the *hypothesis of parallelism*, that is, to assume that such and such a pair of lines in the picture represents lines that are parallel to each other in the scene. For example, here is a geometric method that relies on the identification of a drawing as a perspectival representation of a rectangular parallelepiped (a box with six rectangular faces).

[If the box shown in Figure 6-2 is assumed to be upright, i.e., its top and bottom faces are assumed to be horizontal, then we must assume a tilted picture plane (as if we were looking at the box from above). Because the picture plane is neither parallel nor orthogonal to any of the box's faces, there are three vanishing points. The two horizontal vanishing points V' and V'' are conjugate, as is the vertical vanishing point V''' with each of the other ones. Each pair of conjugate vanishing points defines the diameter of a sphere that passes through the center of projection, which we wish to find. (The diameters of the three spheres form a triangle, $V'V''V'''$, and the intersection of each sphere with the picture plane is a circle; in Figure 6-2 we show only half of each circle). Because the three spheres pass through the center of projection, the single point they share must be the center of projection we are looking for. Or, to put it in somewhat different terms, the center of projection must be at the point of intersection of the three circles formed by the intersections of the three spheres with each other. But to find this point,

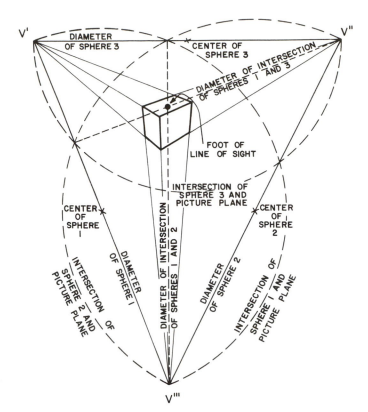

Figure 6-2. Perspective drawing of a figure and determination of center of projection

we need only determine the point of intersection of *two* of these circles. First we note that these circles define planes perpendicular to the picture plane. Thus the line of sight (that is, the principal ray) must be the intersection of these two planes. The diameters of two of the sphere-intersect circles are shown in Figure 6-2; the point at which the diameters intersect is the foot of the line of sight (that is, the intersection of the principal ray with the picture plane). To find the center of projection we need only erect a perpendicular to the picture plane from the foot of the line of sight. To find the distance of the center of projection along this line, we draw one of the sphere-intersect circles, on its diameter we mark the foot of the line of sight, and at that point we erect a perpendicular to the diameter; the perpendicular intersects the circle at the center of projection, at a distance equal to the distance of the center of projection from the picture plane.]

We have just gone through the steps for finding the center of projection of the most elaborate type of perspectival arrangement, three-point perspective. In general, if one wants to find the center of projection of perspectival pictures, one always needs more than one pair of conjugate

90

vanishing points. For instance, in the case of the *construzione legittima* (Figure 1-12), often referred to as one-point perspective, all the sides of box-like objects (interiors of rooms or exteriors of buildings) are either parallel or orthogonal to the picture plane. The vanishing point of the orthogonals is the foot of the line of sight (it plays the role of a pair of conjugate vanishing points). To determine the distance of the center of projection, it is necessary to find another pair of conjugate vanishing points, that is, the so-called distance points (at which the diagonals of a checkerboard pavement converge). Or, consider the somewhat more complicated case of oblique perspective, sometimes called two-point perspective, in which the tops and bottoms of boxes are horizontal (or, more precisely, orthogonal to the picture plane), but the other faces are neither parallel nor orthogonal to the picture plane. To find the center of projection in this case, we must have in the picture at least two boxes whose orientations are different; that is, their sides are not parallel. Then we have two pairs of conjugate vanishing points with which we can find the center of projection.[2]

Let me remind the reader how the question of finding the center of projection came up: We were inquiring why the surface of the picture had to be perceptible for perspective to be robust; in the geometric analysis just concluded, we saw that to find the center of projection we have to construct a perpendicular to the picture plane. Now to erect a perpendicular to the surface of the picture, that surface must be visible. If we assume that the visual system performs an analysis that is analogous to these geometric constructions, then we should not be surprised to observe that when the surface is not visible, as in Pozzo's ceiling, the robustness of perspective is lost. If you do not look at the ceiling from the yellow disk that tells you where to stand for your eye to be at the center of projection, the painted architecture looks lopsided and about to tumble. Pirenne summarizes this point in the following words:

---

[2] La Gournerie (1884, Book VI, Chapter 1), Olmer (1949), and Adams (1972) discuss such procedures.

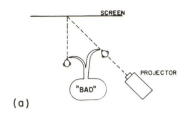

(a)

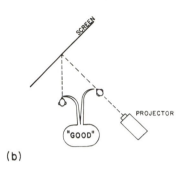

(b)

Figure 6-3. If magic lantern will not come to body's eye, mind's eye must go to magic lantern. (a) When a transparency is projected onto a plane not parallel to plane of transparency, it will look distorted from all vantage points. (b) When a transparency is projected onto a plane parallel to plane of transparency, it will not look distorted from any vantage point (except very extreme ones).

When the shape and the position of the picture surface can be seen, an unconscious psychological process of compensation takes place, which restores the correct view when the picture is viewed from the wrong position. In the case of Pozzo's ceilings, on the other hand, the painted surface is 'invisible' and striking deformations are seen. (1970, p. 99)[3]

Further evidence on the crucial role of the perception of the texture of the picture plane in making possible the robustness of perspective can be obtained by carrying out a very simple experiment. Suppose you want to show slides to an audience, and you are forced to place the projector on one side of the room. How should you place the screen: Should you have the screen face the people in the middle of the room, or should you set up the screen to face the projector? The intuitive solution to this problem is the former. We are uncomfortable in turning the screen away from the spectators; we feel we are not giving them the best possible chance to see the pictures, for, we think, they will look distorted. However, the correct solution is the nonintuitive one: Always set up the screen to be perpendicular to the projector; otherwise the picture will look distorted to everyone in the audience. The explanation for this surprising rule of thumb is simple (see Figure 6-3): We have argued that viewers normally feel that their mind's eye is on a perpendicular to the picture plane, erected at the foot of the principal ray. Let us assume, for the sake of simplicity, that a photograph of a natural scene is being projected. Under optimal viewing conditions, the screen is at a right angle to the optical axis of the projector, and the spectator is very close to the optical axis of the projector. Because most slides are not cropped, the center of the slide can be taken as the center of projection; on that point, a line perpendicular to the picture plane is erected and the viewer feels that his or her mind's eye is on that line, which happens to coincide with the optical axis of the projector, and hence no distortion is experienced. In fact, as long as the optical axis of the projector remains at

---

[3] This theory was developed by Pirenne on the basis of a suggestion made by Albert Einstein in a letter written in 1955.

92

*Figure 6-4. Photograph of a photo-graph (*Time, *March 29, 1968)*

right angles to the screen, the mind's eye will fall on that axis. However, if the screen is tilted relative to the optical axis of the projector, the viewer will locate his or her mind's eye at a point away from the optical axis of the projector and will perceive a distorted picture.

The account I have given of our preference for the positioning of projectors also holds for a phenomenon pointed out by Pirenne (1970, pp. 96–9): If we look at a photograph of a scene that has a photograph in it (such as Figure 6-4), the scene will not appear to be distorted regardless of the

93

point from which we look at the photograph. But unless the photograph in the scene is parallel to the picture plane, it will appear to be flat and distorted from all points of view. It will be seen only as a picture and it will not have the vividness of depth that the scene it belongs to may have. This is an example of the operation of a mechanism of compensation for the viewer's position in space vis-à-vis the picture's center of projection: It suggests that the compensation requires the viewer to be able to perceive the surface of the picture. But in what sense does one not perceive the surface of the photograph in the photograph? In Figure 6-4, we can immediately see that we would have to move our viewpoint to the right in order to see the poster of Nixon frontally. Thus, strictly speaking, we can see the orientation of the surface of the distorted photograph. Why then is it distorted? I believe there are two reasons for this.

First, we can only compensate for one surface at a time. Photocopy Figure 6-5 and fold the copy along the dotted line to form a 90-degree angle and stand it on a surface in front of you. Prop up an unfolded copy of Figure 6-6 next to it. Now compare what happens to the two pictures as you shake your head from side to side. The distortion observed in the folded picture when we move in front of it is striking, whereas there is practically none when we move in front of the flat one. Why is this the case? Presumably, because the folded picture consists of two planes and the flat one consists of just one; and because we can only compensate for one plane at a time. No research has been done on the way we compensate for changes in viewing position when we look at a folded version of Figure 6-5: Do we compensate for one side of the diptych and therefore see the distortion in the other? Or do we attempt to perform a compromise compensation that cannot compensate for the changes in our position vis-à-vis either surface?

The second reason we perceive the distortion of the photograph in the photograph is that we are not free to choose which surface will control the process of compensation: In this picture, there is a primary surface and a secondary

94

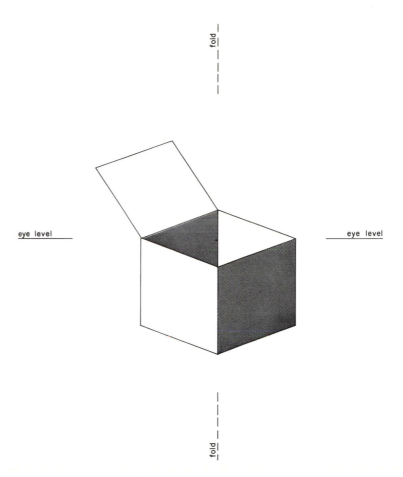

fold

eye level   eye level

fold

Figure 6-5. Photocopy this page. Fold copy along dotted line so that the two sides form a right angle. Prop up sheet so that horizontal line is at eye level. Compare amount of distortion you perceive in shape of cube when you move your head right and left to distortion you see in Figure 6-6.

surface (perhaps unlike the example in Figure 6-5, in which there may be two surfaces equally demanding of compensation). Presumably, there are more cues that tell us that the primary surface is a representation of a scene, such as perceptibility of surface texture and of a frame, than exist for the photograph represented in it.

Although we have made some progress in our inquiry into the robustness of perspective, we have yet to understand how the visual system identifies which angles in the picture represent right angles in the scene, which is (as we have seen earlier in this chapter) a precondition for locating the center of projection. Because the image of a right angle can run anywhere from 0 degrees to 180 degrees, drawings of right angles have no particular signature, and therefore they can be identified only by some more elaborate pro-

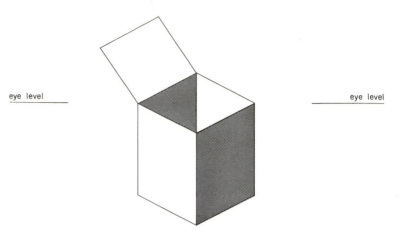

eye level   eye level

Figure 6-6. This drawing corresponds to what you can see in Figure 6-5 when picture is folded to form a 90-degree angle and your eye is on a bisector of that angle.

cedure. There are two views on the nature of this procedure. According to the first view, right angles are identified by first recognizing the objects in which they are embedded. For instance, with respect to Figure 4-1, such an approach would assume that the visual system first recognizes that the picture represents a building and then identifies the features likely to represent right angles. According to the second view, right angles are recognized by first recognizing rectangular corners (i.e., the concurrence of three lines at a point so that all the angles formed are right angles) in which they are embedded. This is possible because, as we will presently see, rectangular corners do have a signature.

The first view, the perception of right angles by an appeal to the semantics of the represented scene, is exemplified by the trapezoidal room created by Adalbert Ames, Jr. This is a room whose plan is shown in Figure 6-7, which looks like a rectangular room to those looking at it through the peephole. Here there is no dilemma. There is ambiguity, however: For an immobile viewer, the visible features of the room are compatible with many possible rooms, including the one the typical viewer reports seeing, which is rectangular, and illusory. But now bring two people into the room; they are at different distances from people into the room; they are at different distances from the observer looking through the peephole and so subtend different visual angles. *Now* we have a dilemma: If the people are seen equal in height, they must be at different

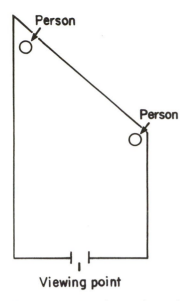

Figure 6-7. Plan of Ames distorted room

distances, and because their backs are against the rear wall, the rear wall cannot be perpendicular to the side walls. On the other horn of the dilemma, if the room is still mistakenly seen as a normal rectangular room, then – so goes the unconscious inference – the people must be at equal distances from the observer; but because they subtend different visual angles, they must differ in height. As may be seen in Figure 6-8, when the viewer is faced with a choice between seeing an oddly shaped room and seeing two adults differ dramatically in height, the latter is chosen. We choose to see grotesque differences in height rather than a distorted room possibly because sizes of human beings vary more in our experience than the angles of room corners. Such an explanation tacitly assumes that the viewer first unconsciously recognizes that the scene represents a room; and because a room implies right angles, the viewer then unconsciously resolves the dilemma of the Ames room by choosing rectangularity over equal heads, which assumes that the semantic interpretation of the scene as a room precedes and determines the interpretation of its features.

In other words, our familiarity with an object depicted in a picture may be sufficient to determine its perceived shape. We do not know whether we perceive the Ames room as we do because of our familiarity with rectangular rooms, but Perkins and Cooper (1980) have provided us with an elegant demonstration that leads us to conclude

Figure 6-8. Distorted room as seen by subject

97

Figure 6-9. Views of John Hancock Tower, Boston, that satisfy (left) and that do not satisfy (right) Perkins's laws

that familiarity with the object is probably not critical in perceiving rectangularity in real objects. In Figure 6-9, we see two views of the John Hancock Tower in Boston, one of which appears to have a rectangular cross section, the other of which appears strangely distorted. This impression is not confined to looking at *pictures* of the tower: One gets the same impression by looking at it from the vantage points of these pictures. The cross section of the building is actually a parallelogram, and so the view that appears distorted (because it does not fit our preconceptions about the shapes of buildings) is in fact the more veridical one. So we conclude that our knowledge of architecture does not override the effect of purely optical changes in the projection of an object.

Furthermore, as Perkins and Cooper (1980) have shown, the hypothesis that the resolution of the dilemma of perspective in favor of rectangularity is conditioned by semantics, that is to say by object or scene recognition, is

98

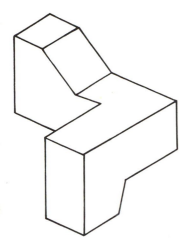

Figure 6-10. Drawing of unfamiliar object that we perceive to have right angles

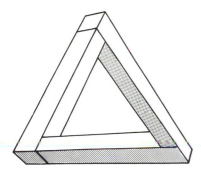

Figure 6-11. Drawing of impossible object that we perceive to have right angles

dealt a blow by the observation that the objects in Figures 6-10 and 6-11 appear to have right angles even though they are not familiar; indeed, the object in Figure 6-11 is as unfamiliar as an object can get – it is impossible. These drawings show that the visual system need not and probably does not appeal to semantics in order to resolve the dilemma of perspective.

Thus we are led to the alternative to semantics: that an angle in a picture is seen as a representation of a right angle only when it is perceived as a part of a representation of a rectangular corner. To understand how this can be done, we must consider *junctures*, the local features that represent the vertices of objects that have straight edges. Figure 6-12 is the drawing of a cube in which two of the junctures have been labeled, for obvious reasons, *fork* and *arrow* junctures. Perkins (1968, 1972, 1973) formulated the following laws:

Perkins's first law. A fork juncture is perceived as the vertex of a cube if and only if the measure of each of the three angles is greater than 90 degrees.

Perkins's second law. An arrow juncture is perceived as the vertex of a cube if and only if the measure of each of the two angles is less than 90 degrees and the sum of their measures is greater than 90 degrees.

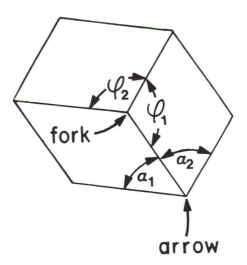

Figure 6-12. Drawing of cube indicating angles comprising fork *juncture and* arrow *juncture*

99

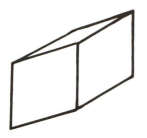

Figure 6-13. Drawing of three-dimensional object that does not look rectangular and does not obey Perkins's laws

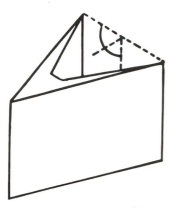

Figure 6-14. Shape that is seen as rectangular prism with mirror-symmetric, irregular, pentagonal cross section because it obeys an extension of Perkins's second law.

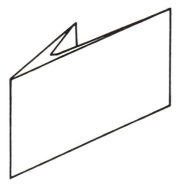

Figure 6-15. Figure that is not seen to have regularity of Figure 6-14 because it does not obey extension of Perkins's laws

Figure 6-10 obeys Perkins's laws, whereas the form in Figure 6-13 does not; the former looks rectangular, the latter does not. Perkins's laws can be extended to junctures that are not themselves rectangular, but that are part of bodies that can be decomposed into two congruent bodies, each of which has a rectangular juncture. Figure 6-14 shows an object that is seen as a rectangular prism with a mirror-symmetric irregular pentagonal cross section. We have added auxiliary lines to the drawing to indicate the plane of symmetry and a line joining two symmetric vertices of the cross section. The arrow juncture obtained in the process of drawing these auxiliary lines satisfies Perkins's second law and is therefore seen as the vertex of a cube, which implies the other perceived features. Figure 6-15, on the other hand, does not look symmetric, and there is some question regarding whether its upper surface looks orthogonal to the sides.

These laws, with their emphases on 90-degree angles in the picture, are related to a special case of central projection, in which the center of projection is infinitely distant from the picture plane. In this type of projection, called *parallel projection*, there is no center of projection and the projecting rays (Figure 1-2) are parallel, there is no horizon line on which parallel lines converge at vanishing points, and parallel lines in the scene are depicted as parallel lines in the picture. It turns out that Perkins's laws are not just laws of perception: They also state the possible *parallel* projections of rectangular vertices. As we will see presently, Perkins's laws are not generally applicable to central projection. That is, certain geometrically correct central projections give rise to pictures that violate Perkins's laws and therefore do not look right.

Perkins's laws were independently discovered by Roger N. Shepard and Elizabeth Smith in an experiment[4] that

The Shepard and Smith experiment was carried out in 1971 and published in 1972 (Shepard, 1981). Perkins (1972) published a similar experiment in 1972. The major difference between these experiments is that Shepard and Smith also studied the perception of vertices of non-rectangular objects, whereas Perkins confined himself to rectangular vertices. Other relevant research is Cooper (1977), Perkins (1973), and Perkins and Cooper (1980).

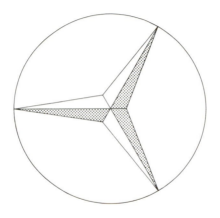

Figure 6-16. Three objects that sub-jects were asked to compare to draw-ings. Upper panel: Mercedes-Benz equiangle trademark (rotated 90 de-grees); middle panel: vertex of a cube; lower panel: vertex of a tetra-hedron. The pictures of these objects all contain a "fork" (see Figure 6-17), for which (roughly)
$\theta_1 = \theta_2 = 120$ *degrees.*

studied the perception of vertices of cubes, tetrahedrons (in which three edges meet at 60-degree angles), and plane patterns like the Mercedes-Benz equiangle trademark (in which three lines in a plane meet at 120-degree angles). Figure 6-16 shows the three objects studied. Shepard and

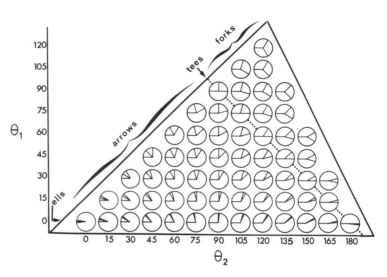

Figure 6-17. Upper right: *If one radius, r₁, is fixed, two angles can specify orientation of the other two radii.* θ₁ *is measure of angle between r₁ and r₂;* θ₂ *is measure of angle between r₂ and r₃. Lower left: Half the forms (remaining forms are mirror images of forms shown here) used in experiment.* Forks *are forms for which* θ₁ + θ₂ > 180°; tees *are forms for which* θ₁ + θ₂ = 180°; arrows *are forms for which* θ₁ + θ₂ < 180°; *and ells are forms for which* θ₁ *or* θ₂ = 0° *(angles labeled 0° here are small angles, measuring roughly 7.5°, so as to ensure that there will always be three lines in each form).*

Smith created 122 patterns, each of which was a circle with three radii (see Figure 6-17). The orientation of one of the radii was held fixed: It was always horizontal. Each pattern differed from others in the disposition of the other two radii; subjects were asked to say of each pattern whether it was an acceptable drawing of each of the three objects studied.

Figure 6-18 shows the results of the experiment. The data of greatest interest to us are those shown in panel B: For all the stimuli that obeyed Perkins's laws, more than 50 percent of the subjects accepted the pattern as the representation of the vertex of a cube; for all the stimuli that violated Perkins's laws, almost no subjects accepted the pattern as a representation of the vertex of a cube.

Let us recapitulate: A perceiver is faced with the dilemma of perspective when a picture drawn in perspective is seen from a vantage point other than the center of projection.

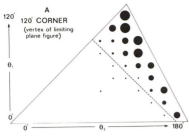

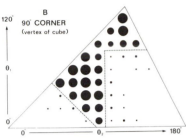

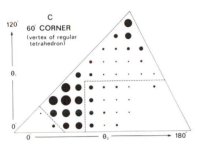

Figure 6-18. Proportion of subjects accepting each pattern as representing Mercedes-Benz equiangle (panel A), vertex of cube (panel B), and vertex of tetrahedron (panel C). Areas of disks in three panels (whose organization parallels that in Figure 6-17) represent proportion of subjects accepting patterns as projections of three types of objects. Dashed boundaries in three panels delimit stimuli that are possible parallel projections of each type of object. In panel B, these boundaries also delimit stimuli that obey Perkins's laws.

The perceiver must either assume that the center of projection coincides with the perceiver's vantage point, in which case the proper interpretation of the scene will change with each change of vantage point, or the perceiver must infer the location of the center of projection and reconstruct the proper scene as it would be seen from that point. Because we have seen that perspective is robust in the face of changing vantage points, the latter must be the case. Furthermore, because inferring the location of the center of projection seems to require an assumption that the objects represented are rectangular, we examined the question of the perception of rectangularity of corners in pictures. We discussed two possibilities: that the perception of rectangularity is based on familiarity with the sorts of objects represented and that rectangularity is based on geometric rules that apply to the configuration of line junctures that represent right-angled vertices. We concluded in favor of the latter.

7

The bounds of perspective: marginal distortions

. . . human kind
Cannot bear very much reality.
> T. S. Eliot, from "Burnt Norton," 1935 (Eliot, 1963, p. 190)

We turn now to a class of pictures that are unacceptable because they do not conform to the robustness of perspective, that is, they look distorted to all viewers except those who look at the picture from the center of projection. The existence of such pictures, as we shall see, constrains central projection, forcing artists to compromise in their methods of representing scenes. The upper-right-hand panel of Figure 7-1 looks distorted from all vantage points except the center of projection, just over an inch away from the page, too close to focus on the lines; the drawing in the lower-left-hand panel does not look distorted from any vantage point. The two pictures differ in the distance of the center of projection from the image plane, which is equivalent to a difference in visual angle subtended by the scene: The first subtends 102 degrees, whereas the second subtends only 19 degrees. It is not known how big the visual angle can be before such distortions, called *marginal distortions*, appear in pictures made using central perspective. Olmer, in his extensive treatise on perspective, *Perspective Artistique* (2 vols.: 1943, 1949), reviewed the recommendations of artists and writers on perspective and concluded in favor of a horizontal visual angle of 37 degrees (and a vertical visual angle of 28 degrees), which he calls *perspective normale*. In Figures 7-2 and 7-3, he compares an

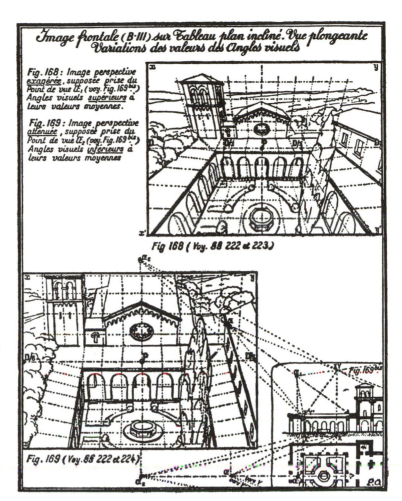

Fig 168 (Voy. §§ 222 et 223.)

Fig. 169 (Voy. §§ 222 et 224.)

Figure 7-1. Two central projections of a church and cloister. In lower-right-hand panel (labeled Fig. 169bis) is a plan and elevation of the scene, showing OE$_1$, the center of projection used to draw upper-right-hand panel (labeled Fig. 168), and OE$_2$, center of projection for lower-left-hand panel (labeled Fig. 169). Width of scene in Fig. 168 subtends a visual angle of 102 degrees from center of projection; width of scene in Fig. 169 subtends 19 degrees.

array of cubes drawn in "normal perspective" with an array of cubes drawn in what he calls *perspective exagerée*. In the latter drawing, he shows that in a central area subtending 37 degrees cubes are not distorted. In an even more dramatic example (Figure 7-4), he shows that outside the frame $xyx'y'$, which encompasses what he calls the normal visual field (37 degrees by 28 degrees), the cubes are seen as distorted.

We know that fields exceeding a critical extent cannot be properly perceived without moving one's eyes. Imagine a horse standing some distance away presenting his flank to you. Now image yourself moving toward the horse: As you move closer to the horse, it looms larger; there will come a point when you are so close that you will not

105

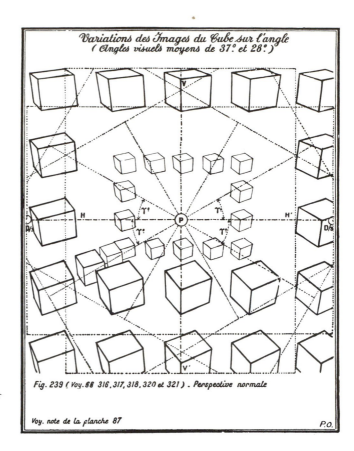

Figure 239 (Voy. §§ 316, 317, 318, 320 et 321) . Perspective normale

Voy. note de la planche 87   P.O.

Figure 7-2. Variations of pictures of oblique cubes seen under normal perspective

be able to see all of it at the same time, unless you move your eyes or turn your head. Furthermore, if you are asked to visualize something, such as an animal, seen at a large distance, and to imagine yourself moving toward it, there will come a point when you will imagine yourself so close to the thing you are visualizing that it seems to "overflow" your "mental screen." Estimates of the size of the visual field that we can encompass in focal attention are difficult to obtain. Using variants on the mental imagery procedure just described, Steven Kosslyn (1978) obtained estimates ranging from 13 to 50 degrees, which bracket Olmer's estimate of the normal visual field.

A somewhat different procedure, developed by A. Sanders (1963, Experiment 3, pp. 49–52), required a subject to look at a fixation point where a column consisting of either four or five lights would appear, while simultaneously, to the right of the fixated column of lights, another of column

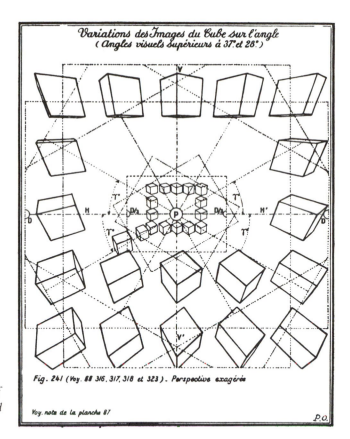

Voy. note de la planche 87

P.O.

Figure 7-3. Variations of pictures of oblique cubes seen under exaggerated perspective

of lights would appear, also consisting of four or five lights (Figure 7-5). The angular distance between the two displays varied from 19 to 94 degrees. Furthermore, there were two viewing conditions: one in which subjects were allowed to move their eyes to scan the display, and one in which they were instructed to keep their eyes on the location of the left column. The subject's task was to press one of four keys as quickly as possible after the two columns of lights were turned on. One key meant that both columns consisted of four lights, a second key meant that both had five, and the remaining two keys covered the remaining two possibilities of unequal numbers in the two columns. The median reaction times of two subjects are shown in Figure 7-6. First, look at the reaction times represented by the filled circles and summarized by the broken curve (condition I: eye movements forbidden). The larger the display angle, the longer the reaction time; beyond 34

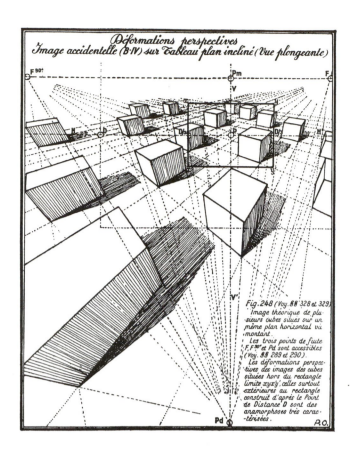

Figure 7-4. Marginal distortions in picture of array of cubes seen from above

degrees, the task was impossible. Second, look at the reaction times represented by unfilled circles and summarized by the solid curve (condition II: eye movements required). Up to about 30 degrees, reaction times were longer than those obtained in the absence of eye movements, suggesting that eye movements were not necessary to see the right-hand column for smaller visual angles. This then is an estimate of the size of the field encompassed by the stationary eye. This estimate of the field normally captured by a glance is not inconsistent with Olmer's normal visual field.

The most impressive confirmation of our attempt to link the extent of Olmer's normal visual field for perspective drawings with the extent of what we can encompass in a single glance is provided by an experiment done by Finke and Kurtzman (1981). Imagine that you are looking at Figure 7-7 and that you are handed a pointer with a red

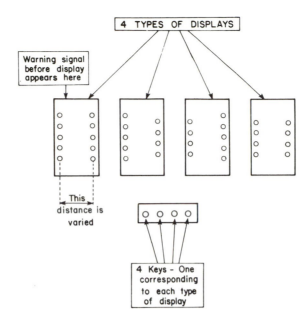

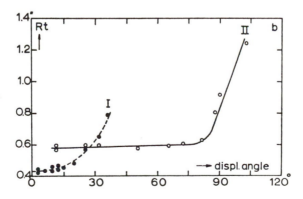

Figure 7-5. Four displays and response keys used by Sanders (1963)

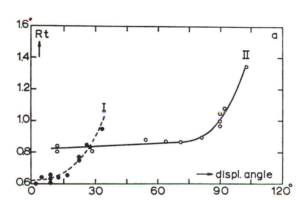

Figure 7-6. Median reaction time (in seconds) as a function of display angle and fixation conditions: Condition I: Eyes immobile, fixating left column (filled circles, broken line). Condition II: Eye movements required (blank circles, solid line). Panels a and b represent data of two subjects.

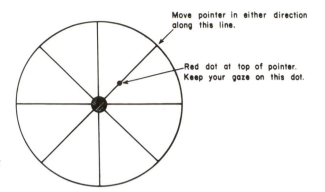

Figure 7-7. Display used by Finke and Kurtzman (1981) to measure extent of visual field in imagery and perception

dot on its tip and are asked to move it up along the diagonal line while keeping your eyes on the red dot. As you move the pointer and your gaze away from the center of the circle, it becomes gradually more difficult to discriminate the two sets of stripes, until you cannot tell that there are two distinct sets. The distance from the center at which this loss occurs is taken as an estimate of the boundary of the visual field. If the pattern is turned 45 degrees clockwise and the observer is asked to move the pointer and his eyes rightward along the *horizontal* line, the boundary is found somewhat further from the center of the circle. If the procedure is repeated six more times, once for each remaining radial line, a rough estimate of the shape of the visual field can be obtained.

The size of the visual field estimated by this procedure varies with changes in the number of bars per inch: The higher the density of bars in the central pattern, the sooner the observer will report that the pattern has melted into a blur. The widest patterns used gave a field of 35 by 28 degrees, gratifyingly close to Olmer's estimate.[1] This correspondence suggests that we are comfortable with perspective drawings only if the scene they encompass does not subtend a visual angle greater than we would normally encompass in our visual field.

---

[1] Finke and Kurtzman went further. They also trained observers to *imagine* the grating and then asked them to move their eyes away from the position of the imagined pattern until it was too blurred to be seen by the mind's eye. The results were extremely close to the results obtained for perceived patterns.

110

To find what it is in perspective pictures subtending a large visual angle that causes us to reject them, let us look back at Olmer's figures, which subtend large visual angles (Figures 7-3 and 7-4): Not all the cubes that fall outside the interior frame that bounds Olmer's normal visual field (between the two points D/3 in Figure 7-3, and within the rectangle $xx'\gamma\gamma'$ in Figure 7-4) look equally distorted. In Figure 7-4, for instance, compare the cube just below the line $x'\gamma'$ to the cube just to the left of x'. The former looks considerably more distorted than the latter; it violates Perkins's law for forks, one of the angles of the fork being less than 90 degrees. Only the cubes that violate Perkins's laws look distorted; the others do not. Therefore, perhaps it is not the wide angle of the view per se, but rather local features of the depictions, that cause these pictures to look distorted.

We are now in a position to understand the connection between Perkins's laws and the limited size of our visual field. We have seen from Olmer's drawings that the perspective drawings of rectangular objects are likely to violate Perkins's laws only when they fall outside a field that subtends 37 degrees by 28 degrees. We have also seen that, because our visual field subtends about 37 degrees by 28 degrees, we are unlikely to perceive objects in our environment that fall outside such a field. In other words, the projections of objects that fall within our field of view all obey Perkins's laws. Because Perkins's laws are very simple, we may notice their violation in pictures only because they constitute a striking deviation from what we are accustomed to see and not because of the relation of Perkins's laws to parallel projection, which we observed in Chapter 6.[2]

---

[2] Hagen and Elliott (1976) have made unwarranted claims in favor of the hypothesis that parallel projection is more natural than central projection (and predates it by about two millennia). They showed subjects pictures of 7 different objects (2 cubes and 5 regular pentagonal right prisms) using 6 different degrees of "perspective convergence from conical (traditional linear perspective) to axonometric (parallel) projection" (p. 481). They claim that "for a given object of fixed dimension observed from a fixed station point, a family of perspective views may be generated . . . "(p. 481). Among the problems that invalidate this experiment and

Up to this point, we have been discussing the marginal distortion of right angles. Figure 7-8 (the panel labeled Fig. 243) shows that the correct central projection of a sphere that is not centered on the principal ray is an ellipse. Nevertheless, if the projectively correct ellipses were substituted for the circles with which Raphael represented the spheres in his *School of Athens*[3] (Figure 7-9 and the detail in Figure 7-10), they would not look like spheres (unless the fresco were viewed through a peephole at the center of projection). This misperception of the correct projection of a sphere is a marginal distortion very much like the misperception of projectively correct representations of the vertices of cubes when they are outside the area of normal perspective (because they are likely to violate Perkins's laws). There is, however, one major difference: A cube can be anywhere within the area of normal perspective and still look like a cube; a sphere that is not on the principal ray will look distorted. The visual system, so tolerant of

Footnote 2 (cont.)

the authors' interpretation of it, I will mention four: (*1*) Changes in convergence are equivalent to changes in the location of the center of projection (the station point). It is meaningless to speak of a change in convergence without a concomitant change in the center of projection. (*2*) In their experiment, not all the pictures that were meant to depict different projections of one object showed the same number of the object's faces, and many of these pictures were degenerate to the extent that they precluded the recognition of the object (for example, one picture of a cube was a rectangle divided into two rectangles by a vertical line). At least 10 of the 42 pictures suffered from such extreme degeneracy, and 4 of the 7 objects depicted had at least 1 degenerate picture. Because the purported differences in "degree of perspective convergence" were inextricably confounded with large variations in the amount of visual information these pictures conveyed, it is impossible to interpret subjects' preferences for some of the representations. (*3*) Of the 3 objects whose 6 pictures did not include cases of extreme degeneracy, 1 (the most convergent central projection of a cube, labeled *A* in their Figure 1) was a borderline violation of Perkins's law; hence it was fated to be rejected by subjects, but not because of their putative preference for parallel projection. (*4*) Among the 3 objects whose pictures did not include cases of degeneracy, only 1 yielded data unequivocally in support of Hagen and Elliott's conclusion that parallel-perspective drawings were the most natural or realistic drawings.

An experiment credited by Pirenne (1970, p. 122) to La Gournerie (1859, p. 170). The second edition of La Gournerie's treatise (1884) does not mention the experiment.

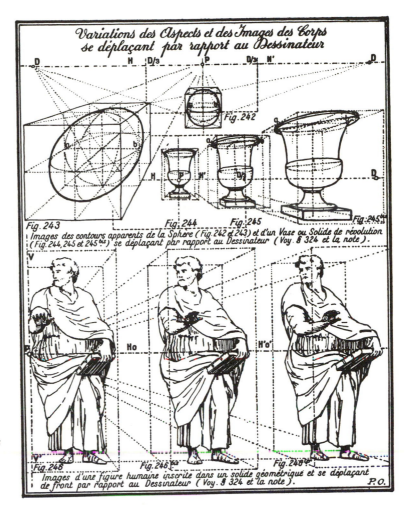

Figure 7-8. Panel [Fig.] 242: Central projection of sphere centered on principal ray is a circle. Panel 243: Central projection of sphere not on principal ray is an ellipse and does not look like a sphere. Panels 246-246ter: Three projections of Raphael's Aristotle (see Figure 7-9) as they should be drawn at different displacements to the right of the principal ray.

variations in the representations of vertices of cubes, is completely intolerant of variations in the representations of spheres. As discussed earlier in this chapter, the link between *perspective exagérée* and Perkins's laws is that the latter are a convenient rule of thumb that separate pictures that could represent objects in our normal field of view from those that could not. Vertices of cubes that are on the principal ray vary in their appearance depending on the distance of the center of projection from the picture plane; the projection of a sphere whose center is on the principal ray is always a circle. Furthermore, there is no convenient, easy to perceive, rule of thumb (analogous to Perkins's laws) to separate the unlikely projections of spheres from

Figure 7-9. Raphael, The School of Athens *(1510–1). Fresco. Stanza della Segnatura, Vatican, Rome.*

the likely ones: The difference between the projection of a sphere that falls just within the area of normal perspective and one that falls just outside is a purely quantitative difference in the ratio of the long dimension of an ellipse (major axis) to its shorter dimension (minor axis). As a result, *only circles are considered acceptable projections* of spheres. And because artists have always accepted the primacy of perception over geometry, whenever they represented spheres in their paintings (which was not often), they always represented them as circles. In other words, it is as if whenever a sphere had to be represented, an ad hoc center of projection and a new principal ray (which passed through the center of the sphere) was created.

Just as the correct central projection of a sphere becomes a more elongated ellipse the further the center of the sphere

Figure 7-10. Detail of Figure 7-9 showing Ptolemy, Euclid, and others.

is from the principal ray, the wider the correct central projection of a cylindrical column becomes under these circumstances[4] (see Figure 7-11). This marginal distortion is mostly academic, because I have not found any Renaissance paintings of colonnades that could have been subject to this sort of distortion and were corrected to accord with perception. Nevertheless, Leonardo was aware of the problem, and he correctly pointed out that, although the progressive thickening of the pictures of columns the further they are from the principal ray (and the concomitant nar-

---

[4] This kind of marginal distortion was first discussed by Uccello and analyzed extensively by Leonardo. For a review, see White (1967, Chapter XIV). A more detailed analysis was published in 1774 by Thomas Malton; see Plate 144 (Fig. 34) in Descargues (1977). La Gournerie (1884) also discusses it in detail.

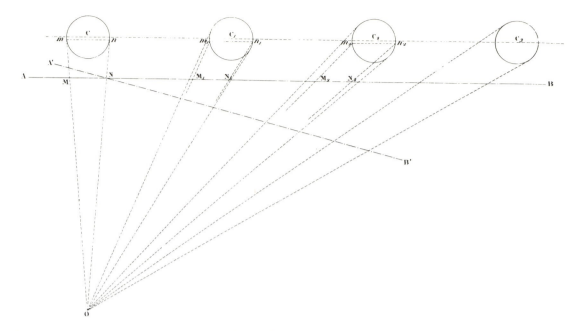

Figure 7-11. Plan of four cylindrical columns, C, C₁, C₂, C₃, projected onto picture plane AB using O as center of projection. Although frontal chords of circular cross sections of the columns (mn, m₁n₁, m₂n₂) project as constants (MN, M₁N₁, M₂N₂), diameters of columns project wider images the further away they are from principal ray.

rowing of the spaces between them) is implied by central projection, this "good" method (as he puts it) is "satisfactory" only if the picture is viewed through a peephole located at the center of projection. He concludes that when the picture "is to be seen by several persons" the only perceptually acceptable solution (which is "the lesser fault," i.e., not as good as using a peephole) is analogous to what Raphael did with the sphere: to ignore the rules of geometry and to represent the columns in the colonnade "in their proper size," that is, with equally wide projections (Leonardo da Vinci, 1970, §544, pp. 326–7).

If spheres and cylinders are treated in a special way by the practice of perspective, it should not come as a surprise that the same is true of human bodies. If we think of the human body as a flattened sphere on top of a flattened cylinder, we can appreciate the distortions its picture undergoes as it is displaced away from the principal axis of the projection. In Figure 7-8, the panels labeled Fig. 246, 246bis, 246ter, Olmer shows three versions of the figure of Aristotle from Raphael's *School of Athens*, successively displaced to the right from the principal ray. Needless to say, artists never complied with this implication of geometry. Let us examine the famous fresco by Paolo Uccello *Sir*

Figure 7-12. Paolo Uccello, Sir
John Hawkwood *(1436). Fresco,
transferred to canvas. Cathedral of
Santa Maria delle Fiore, Florence.*

John Hawkwood to illustrate this most interesting violation
of the geometric rules of central projection (Figure 7-12).
Here is Hartt's description of the work:

[Uccello's] earliest dated painting is the colossal fresco in the
Cathedral of Florence, painted in 1436 on commission from the
officials of the Opera del Duomo, an equestrian monument to
the English condottiere Sir John Hawkwood, known to the Ital-
ians as Giovanni Acuto, to whom a monument in marble had
been promised just before his death in 1394. . . .
  The pedestal rests on a base that is supported by three consoles
. . . The simulated architecture is projected in perspective from

117

a point of view far below the lower border of the fresco, at about eye level of a person standing in the side-aisle.[5] But the horse and rider are seen from a second point of view, at about the middle of the horse's legs. One is tempted to speculate as to why Uccello changed the perspective system. If he had projected the horse and rider from below, in conformity with the pedestal, the observer would have looked up to the horse's belly, and have seen little of the rider but his projecting feet and knees and the underside of his face. But might not Uccello, a lifelong practical joker, have done exactly that? Perhaps at first he did. The officials of the Opera objected to his painting of the horse and rider and compelled him to destroy that section of the fresco and do it over again. The explanation of this oft-noted circumstance[6] may well have been Uccello's view of the great man from below. (1969, pp. 212–13)

John White writes in a similar vein:

The advantages of [using several viewpoints in a single composition] – sometimes even the necessity for it, are shown most obviously in Uccello's Hawkwood . . . A fairly high degree of realism was desirable in frescoes which were substitutes for more expensive marble monuments, and this element of illusion is supplied by the steep foreshortening of the architectural [base].

---

[5] Actually, the present viewing level is near the floor. Hartt is describing the original state of affairs as if it were current.

[6] Described by Pope-Hennessy (1969, p.7) as follows: "On 30 May [1436] Uccello was ordered to replace [Agnolo] Gaddi's fresco [of Hawkwood, commissioned in 1395] with a new fresco in *terra verde* [meaning green earth, a natural earth color], on 28 June he was instructed to efface the horse and rider he had executed on the wall 'because it was not painted as it should be,' on 6 July he was told to make a new attempt, and by the end of August the fresco was complete. The erasure of the first version was due probably to some technical defect in the preparation of the ground, and not, as is often implied, to dissatisfaction with Uccello's cartoon [full-size drawing used for transfer to a wall on which a fresco is to be painted]." I find Pope-Hennessy's attribution of the erasure of the first version to a "technical defect in the preparation of the ground" implausible: Why would there be such a defect in the preparation of the ground of the horse and rider and not a similar defect in the ground of the base? Furthermore, what prompted the erasure of the second version? I think, as I explain later in this chapter, that Uccello had discovered that strict adherence to the laws of perspective made for unacceptable paintings and that he had to compromise twice before the result was acceptable to viewers. I also think that the tolerance of his employers was due to the avant-garde nature of Uccello's application of perspective.

118

On the other hand a worm's eye panorama of a horse's belly and a general's feet can be at best a dubious tribute to his memory. The realism of the low-set viewpoint is therefore restricted to the architecture. In Uccello's fresco there is no foreshortening of the horse or rider . . . (1967, p. 197)

Peter and Linda Murray attribute the effect to Uccello's incompetence:

During the 1430s [Uccello] became fascinated by the new ideas in perspective and foreshortening, although he never really mastered the full implications of the system, which became for him, eventually, no more than another form of elaborate pattern-making. Even when the impact of the new ideas was fresh, his treatment of them was quite arbitrary, as can be seen in the [fresco of] Sir John Hawkwood . . . This has two separate viewpoints, one for the base and another for the horseman . . . ; a similarly irrational approach was also used in his *Four Heads of Prophets* of 1443 in the roundels in the corners of the clock of Florence Cathedral. (1963, pp. 113–14)

In view of our analysis of marginal distortions, I believe that Hartt and White are only partially correct in their analysis of why Uccello chose two inconsistent centers of projection, and, a fortiori, I believe that Murray and Murray err in their attempt to debunk Uccello's mastery of perspective. Hartt and White are mistaken in thinking that, as Hartt puts it, if Uccello "had projected the horse and rider from below, in conformity with the pedestal, the observer would have looked up to the horse's belly, and have seen little of the rider but his projecting feet and knees and the underside of his face." Hartt's and White's analyses are based on a failure to appreciate the importance of the distinction between the central projection of a scene (in our case, the monument) from a low vantage point onto a *vertical* picture plane, and its projection onto a *tilted* picture plane. As long as the picture plane is, on the whole, parallel to the important surfaces of the objects represented, such as the side of the horse, *none of the features of these important surfaces is lost by moving the center of projection.* To better understand this point, let us ask the question in a slightly different way: How would the appearance of the horse and rider have changed had they been depicted in a manner consistent with the projection of the base, that is, from a low vantage point onto a vertical picture plane? It is true that more of the horse's underbelly would be visible in the picture, and that the soles of the figure's boots would be seen, but that is true of any equestrian monument erected on a tall pedestal. But Hartt and White are wrong to think that the horse's underbelly and the figure's soles would be visible to the exclusion of the side of the horse and the side of the rider. That would happen only if the picture plane were tilted, which would not be consistent with Uccello's representation of the base of the statue. I do not think that a representation of the horse and rider that would be consistent with the representation of the base would have been "a dubious tribute" to the general's memory and therefore do not believe that the officials of the Opera del Duomo who viewed the first version of Uccello's fresco were angered by having been the butt of a practical joke (an unlikely action on the part of an aspiring young artist, dependent on further commissions). What is at stake here is marginal distortion: I believe that Uccello's first attempt was a correct central projection of the pedestal, the horse, and the rider, which suffered from extreme marginal distortion; that his second attempt was a partial compromise, which was still afflicted with too much distortion; and that his third attempt – which is the masterpiece we know so well – was perceptually acceptable. Leonardo elevated Uccello's procedure to the level of principle:

In drawing from the round the draughtsman should so place himself that the eye of the figure he is drawing is on a level with his own. This should be done with any head he may have to represent from nature because, without exception, the figures or persons you meet in the streets have their eyes on the same level as your own; and if you place them higher or lower you will see that your drawing will not bear resemblance. (Leonardo da Vinci, 1970, §541, p. 325)

In conclusion, we have seen that nonrectangular bodies that are not on the principal axis of a central projection cause problems for the would-be orthodox user of this sort of projection. In general, such bodies – including humans and animals – are not drawn in accordance with the geometry of central projection. Instead, each body is drawn from a center of projection on a line perpendicular to the picture plane intersecting the picture at a point inside the contour of the body. Only the size of the nonrectangular objects and their position in the two-dimensional space of the picture are subject to the rules of central projection. We have argued in this chapter that this convention of painting reflects the perspectivists' acceptance of the primacy of perception and that central projection is applied principally to architectural settings of scenes. So perspective, as it was practiced by artists, was far from being an inflexible system. Because it was subordinated to perception and because different kinds of objects were made to obey the laws of central projection to different extents, a unifying concept such as Alberti's window cannot do justice to the subtleties and complexities of Renaissance perspective.

Some artists and scholars, who did not recognize the richness and elaborateness of perspective, have thought of it as an awesome monster unleashed on the art of the Renaissance, a geometric system so truculent that it confined the imagination of artists to an inescapable four-square grid. Here, for instance, is how Carlo Carrà wrote in his 1913 manifesto of Futurism, *The Painting of Sounds, Noises, and Odors*:

The old running perspective and trompe l'oeil, a game worthy at most of an academic mind such as Leonardo's, or of a designer of sets for realist melodramas.[7]

The Gestalt psychologist Rudolph Arnheim expresses a similar disdain for perspective in his classic *Art and Visual Perception*:

[Perspective] must distort sizes, shapes, and spatial distances and angles in order to convey depth, thus doing considerable violence not only to the character of the two-dimensional medium but also to the objects in the picture. We understand why the film critic André Bazin has called perspective "the original sin of Western painting." In manipulating objects to foster the illusion of depth, picture-making relinquishes its innocence. . . .

[7] Translation mine (from French). Carrà (1913).

The discovery of central perspective bespoke a dangerous development in Western thought. It marked a scientifically oriented preference for mechanical reproduction and geometrical constructs in place of creative imagery. William Ivins [1973, p. 9] has pointed out that, by no mere coincidence, central perspective was discovered only a few years after the first woodcuts had been printed in Europe. The woodcut established for the European mind the almost completely new principle of mechanical reproduction. It is to the credit of Western artists and their public that despite the lure of mechanical reproduction, imagery has survived as a creation of the human spirit. . . . Nevertheless, the lure of mechanical faithfulness has ever since the Renaissance tempted European art, especially in the mediocre standard output for mass consumption. The old notion of "illusion" as an artistic ideal became a menace to popular taste with the beginnings of the industrial revolution. (1974, pp. 258, 284–5)

Perhaps it is this *mimetophobia*, the morbid fear of slavish imitation, that impelled scholars like Herbert Read, Nelson Goodman, and Rudolph Arnheim, to name a few, to look for flaws in central projection as a method for the representation of space. Let us consider the most sustained critique, by Nelson Goodman in his important book *Languages of Art*. One line of Goodman's attack concentrates on what has been called the *projective surrogate*[8] conception of perspective, namely

that pictorial perspective obeys laws of geometrical optics, and that a picture drawn according to the standard pictorial rules will, under the very abnormal conditions outlined above [viewed with one eye only, through a peephole] deliver a bundle of light rays matching that delivered by the scene portrayed. Only this assumption gives any plausibility at all to the argument from perspective; but the assumption is plainly false. By the pictorial rules, railroad tracks running outward from the eye are drawn converging, but telephone poles (or the edges of a facade) running upward from the eye are drawn parallel. By the 'laws of geometry' the poles should also be drawn converging. (1976, pp. 15–16)

Although criticism along these lines is fairly widespread,[9] it rests on a misunderstanding of the basis of perspective. Goodman erroneously assumes that when one talks about

[8] The term is Gibson's (1954). See Chapter 3.
[9] See, for instance, Winner (1982, pp. 94–5).

the "laws of geometry" one is referring to a law according to which the further an object is from the viewer the smaller the visual angle it subtends, which is correct, but is not the basis of perspective. According to the geometric rules of central projection, the projection of any two lines that are parallel to the picture plane, such as two telephone poles, or the edges of an appropriately oriented facade, will be two parallel lines.

Goodman also developed a second line of attack, which runs as follows:

The source of unending debate over perspective seems to lie in confusion over the pertinent conditions of observation. In Figure [7-13], an observer is on ground level with eye at *a*; at *b, c* is the facade of a tower atop a building; at *d, e* is a picture of the tower facade, drawn in standard perspective and to a scale such that at the indicated distances picture and facade subtend equal angles from *a*. The normal line of vision to the tower is the line *a, f*; looking much higher or lower will leave part of the tower facade out of sight or blurred. Likewise, the normal line of vision to the picture is *a, g*. Now although the picture and facade are parallel, the line *a, g* is perpendicular to the picture, so that vertical parallels in the picture will be projected to the eye as parallel, while the line *a, f* is at an angle to the facade so that vertical parallels there will be projected to the eye as converging

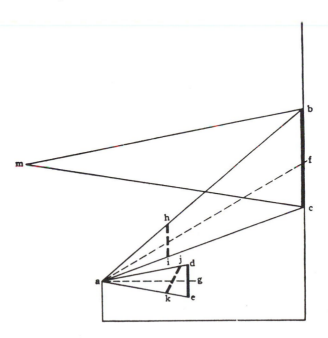

Figure 7-13. Diagram illustrating argument about perspective made by Goodman

upward. We might try to make picture and facade deliver matching bundles of light rays to the eye by either (1) moving the picture upward to the position *h, i,* or (2) tilting it to position *j, k,* or (3) looking at the picture from *a* but at the tower from *m,* some stories up. In the first two cases, since the picture must also be nearer the eye to subtend the same angle, the scale will be wrong for lateral (left–right) dimensions. What is more important, none of these three conditions of observation is anywhere near normal. We do not usually hang pictures far above eye level, or tilt them drastically bottom toward us, or elevate ourselves at will to look squarely at towers. With eye and picture in normal position, the bundle of light rays delivered to the eye by the picture drawn in standard perspective is very different from the bundle delivered by the facade. (1976, pp. 17–19)

Here Goodman makes several errors. No one after Brunelleschi ever tried to "make picture and facade deliver matching bundles of light rays to the eye" in situ, even though it is very easy, in principle, to do so. What some may want to claim for perspective (and I am one of them, though with much hedging) is that, by using it, one can create a picture that, if viewed from the center of projection, will deliver a bundle of light rays to the eye that matches *one* bundle of rays delivered by the scene viewed from one vantage point.

For the sake of argument, let us use Goodman's strict notion of matching. Because Goodman does not tell us where the picture plane was when the picture was made, we must guess. It could not have been at *d, e,* because *a* cannot be the center of projection that would make *d, e,* a picture of *b, c.* If it was at *h, i,* then the perspective belongs to the same rare class as the base in Uccello's *Hawkwood* (Figure 7-12) and Mantegna's *Saint James Led to Execution,* which we will discuss in the next chapter (Figure 8-7). If the artist who created such a picture using central projection also wants the viewer to be able to see it from the center of projection (as Mantegna apparently did), he will place the picture above eye level, notwithstanding Goodman's protestations that such things are not done. If the picture plane was at the height of *m, f,* then it was the artist who must have elevated himself to paint the tower as it is seen squarely, and the only way to match the bundles of

124

light rays from the facade and the picture exactly is to elevate the viewer to the height of the center of projection. The third possibility is one not hinted at by Goodman, and it is the solution to his problem: Suppose that when the picture was drawn the picture plane was perpendicular to *a, f.* Then, when the picture was eventually moved to its "normal" position (according to Goodman) at *d, e,* it would deliver a bundle of light rays matching the one delivered by the facade.

Goodman mistakenly constrained perspective to pictures projected onto vertical picture planes and hung at the height of the eye, but he allowed the height of the center of projection to be chosen at will. Under these constraints, there are indeed pictures that will not deliver a bundle of light rays to match the one delivered by the scene. But those are constraints invented by Goodman on the basis of a misinterpretation of the rules of central projection.

Goodman tried to show that the "choice of official rules of perspective [is] whimsical" (1976, p. 19). This is an extremely pregnant way of putting things. By referring to a choice, Goodman suggests a freedom in the selection of rules of pictorial representation that others have denied. By referring to the choice as whimsical, Goodman suggests that the choice was unwise, to say the least. In the first part of this chapter, I made a point not too far removed from Goodman's, namely, that geometry does not rule supreme in the Land of Perspective. However, we stopped far short of agreeing that the rules of pictorial representation are arbitrary and can be chosen freely. In fact, if in the Land of Perspective geometry plays a role analogous to the role played by Congress in the United States, then perception has the function of the Constitution. Whatever is prescribed by the geometry of central projection is tested against its acceptability to perception. If a law is unconstitutional, it is rejected and must be rewritten to accord with perception.

In consequence, the laws of perspective do not coincide with the geometry of central projection. We have noted two ways in which the practice of perspective deviates from central projection: (1) the restriction of the field of perspective pictures to 37 degrees, and (2) the representation of round bodies (spheres, cylinders, human figures) as if the principal ray of the picture ran through them. This procedure does not preclude foreshortening: It is designed to avoid the rather severe marginal distortions that are perceived when such bodies are not very close to the principal ray.

8 Why was the Brunelleschi peephole abandoned?

The objects tingle and the spectator moves
With the objects. But the spectator also moves
With lesser things, with things exteriorized
Out of rigid realists. . . .

> Wallace Stevens, from "An Ordinary Evening in
> New Haven," 1949 (Stevens, 1972, p. 335)

In Figure 8-1, we can see a reconstruction of Brunelleschi's second panel,[1] described by Manetti as follows:

> He made in perspective the piazza of the palace of the Signori of Florence, . . . in such a way that the two faces are seen completely . . . : so that it is a wonderful thing to see what appears. . . . Here it might be said: why did he not make this picture, being of perspective with a hole for the eye, like the little panel from the Duomo towards Santo Giovanni? This arose because the panel of so great a piazza needed to be so big to put in it so many different things, that it could not, like the Santo Giovanni, be held up to the face with one hand, nor the mirror with the other . . . He left it to the direction of the onlookers as happens in all other paintings of all other painters, although the onlooker may not always be discerning. (Trans. by Edgerton, 1975, pp. 127–9)

---

[1] Martin Kemp (personal communication, 1982) has pointed out that this diagram is somewhat misleading. He writes: "The worst of the innacuracies is that the pavement patterns were not orientated as shown. This makes quite different sense of the perspective. The sides of the Piazza are not aligned at right angles as shown."

Figure 8-1. Edgerton's depiction of Brunelleschi's second experiment

Brunelleschi and the painters of the Renaissance abandoned the peepshow not only because it was unwieldly[2] but, I believe, for two deeper reasons: one is the "gimmicky" effect of a peepshow, which transforms it into mere entertainment; the other is the robustness of perspective, which has as its consequence the potential for the creation of extraordinarily powerful psychological effects.

To better understand why a peepshow smacks of gimmickry and mere entertainment, I propose to digress here and analyze the interesting notion of gimmick. Take prestidigitation. Shows of legerdemain are displays of extraordinary virtuosity, incomprehensible to the uninitiated, but which lose much of their charm once the trick is revealed. To be sure, it is always fascinating to look closely at an extraordinarily able performer or artisan demonstrating his or her skill, but a person who has learned the secret of a magic trick cannot watch its performance and still experience the surprise and awe induced by objects seeming to violate the laws of nature. Similarly, to have looked into

[2] It has been suggested that Brunelleschi painted the first panel on a mirror (leaving the upper part of the panel unpainted to reflect the sky and the moving clouds) and that large mirrors were hard to come by in the fifteenth century (Krautheimer, 1974).

128

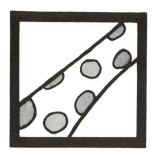

Figure 8-2. Droodle

the back of a perspective cabinet reduces our interest to a curiosity about technique. In this respect, magic and perspective cabinets are like the droodle[3] shown in Figure 8-2. Once you have been given its title,[4] you cannot regain your visual innocence with regard to the picture.

We say of such displays that they are merely entertaining gimmicks. It is true that such objects occasionally prod us into comparing our state of mind before and after our insight into what made us experience the illusion, thus inducing in us a *metaperceptual experience*, which engenders an understanding of the workings of our mind. Nevertheless, they are not primarily designed to do so, nor is that their predominant effect. When illusion is the core of an experience, as it is in magic or perspective cabinets, the work that gives rise to the illusion becomes particularly ephemeral because the mechanics of the illusion rather than the work itself become the focus of the experience. In contrast, to have been backstage at the theater or to have visited an artist's studio very rarely diminishes the power of the finished work of art and often leads us to reflect upon the role of illusion in art.

The claim that works that hinge on illusion are mere gimmicks because of the ephemerality of the experience they afford must be reconciled with the observation that the work of certain influential modern artists suffers from a similar ephemerality. There are two ways to proceed: Either we can accept the complaint of some that much modern art is mere gimmickry, or we can analyze the nature of the ephemerality of certain kinds of modern art and ask what sets it apart from perspective cabinets and the like.

It is a commonplace that modern art evolved by violating accepted norms of "subject matter, but more importantly composition, figure–ground relationships, color, scale, and tactile values" (Burnham, 1973, p. 46). Jack Burnham calls these violations *formal transgressions*. But there is another,

---

[3] "Droodle" is a riddle-like neologism coined by Roger Price that combines the words "doodle" and "riddle."
[4] "Giraffe passing in front of a window."

129

more important, violation of norms that modern artists have engaged in, which Burnham calls *historical transgressions*. These are violations of our conception of the indispensability of the artist's choices and of the artist's voluntary control over the artistic product, on the one hand, and of the indispensability of the physical persistence of the work, on the other. Artists have relinquished voluntary control over the work of art in two ways: by introducing randomness into the process of creation, and by relinquishing key aspects of the fabrication of the work. Randomness has entered the process of creation with the introduction of aleatory methods of pictorial, poetic, and musical composition.[5] An example of this in the pictorial domain is one of Kenneth Martin's aleatory drawings (Figure 8-3).

[The following aleatory process generated Figure 8-3:

An 8-by-8 square grid was numbered from the top in horizontal rows from left to right.

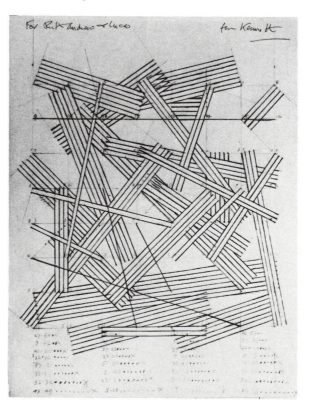

Figure 8-3. Kenneth Martin, Chance and Order Drawing 1981. Pencil. Collection Ruth and Andrew Forge, New Haven, Conn.

[5] On randomness in musical composition, see Cage (1973, pp. 57–61).

130

The numbers from 1 to 64 were written on small cards, which were shuffled. Thirty-two pairs of numbers were picked at random (without replacement, so that no number was drawn twice) in order to determine how each of the 64 intersections in the grid would be connected to one (and only one) other intersection. The 32 pairs were set down in 4 columns of 8.

A single line was drawn for each of the pairs in the top row: $27 \rightarrow 60$, $9 \rightarrow 16$, $63 \rightarrow 41$, and $36 \rightarrow 53$.

Pairs in all the other rows were interpreted in the same fashion, except that sets of parallel lines were drawn, instead of the single lines drawn for the pairs in the top row. Pairs in row 2 were taken as instructions to draw pairs of parallel lines, pairs in row 3 were taken as instructions to draw triplets of parallel lines, and so on.

Consider the pair $3 \rightarrow 42$, the leftmost in the second row. The first of the two parallel lines connected intersections 3 and 42. The second line connecting 3 and 42 lay to the right of the first (assuming the line was oriented toward intersection 42). There is no indication of the procedure used by Martin in this drawing to determine whether the expansion was to be to the right or to the left: Twelve of the 28 multiple connectors expand to the right, and the remainder expand to the left.

This drawing reflects the order in which the lines were drawn by following a rule whereby a set of parallel lines is always interrupted by preexisting sets of lines. For instance, the pair of lines $3 \rightarrow 42$ was drawn before the pairs $43 \rightarrow 33$ and $37 \rightarrow 25$; therefore, the latter seem to be occluded by the former where they happen to intersect. Thus, if each set of lines intersected its immediate precursor (which is not the case: We cannot tell by looking at the drawing the ordinal position of pair $31 \rightarrow 45$ in row 2), the drawing would have 32 distinct layers in depth.

Martin uses the same set of random pairs for several drawings and paintings. For instance, the drawing *Chance and Order X/6* (Martin, 1973) differs in the order of drawing the connecting lines, and in the rule for right or left expansion.]

In addition to the incorporation of randomness into the process of creation, some artists have attempted to undermine the norms that define a work of art by deliberately curtailing the physical life of the work. Thus transitoriness has become (for some) a central characteristic of works of art such as Jean Tinguely's *Homage to New York* (Figure 8-4), a sculpture-machine that was supposed to self-destruct, but didn't (because it broke). John Cage called this attitude toward painting "art as sand painting (art for the now-moment rather than for posterity's museum civilization)" (1973, p. 65). He adds a footnote to "art for the now-moment":

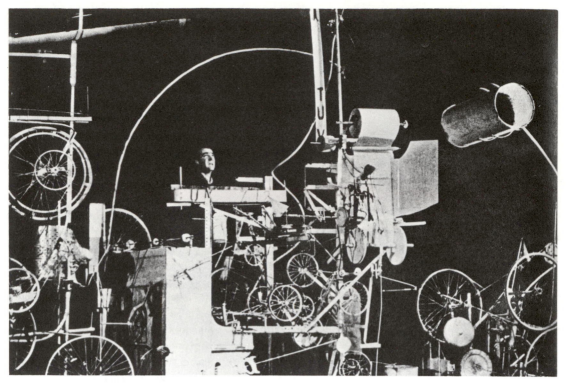

Figure 8-4. Jean Tinguely, Homage to New York. *A self-constructing and self-destroying work of art. Demonstration in sculpture garden of Museum of Modern Art, New York, March 17, 1960.*

This is the very nature of the dance, of the performance, of music, or any other art requiring performance (for this reason, the term "sand painting" is used: there is a tendency in painting (permanent pigments), as in poetry (printing, binding), to be secure in the thingness of a work, and thus to overlook, and place nearly insurmountable obstacles in the path of, instantaneous ecstasy). (1973, p. 65, footnote 10)

Some artists have even circumvented the process of making the work of art. Certain artists did so by using *objets trouvés*, which Marcel Duchamp called Readymades, such as his *Bottlerack* (Figure 8-5). In his fascinating monograph on Duchamp, Octavio Paz writes:

The Readymades are anonymous objects that the artist's gratuitous gesture, the mere fact of choosing them, converts into works of art. At the same time this gesture does away with the notion of art object. The essence of the act is contradiction; it is the plastic equivalent of the pun. As the latter destroys meaning, the former destroys the idea of value. . . .

The Readymade is a criticism of . . . manual art. . . . The artist is not the maker of things; his works are not pieces of workmanship – they are acts. (1981, pp. 21–2, 23–4)

132

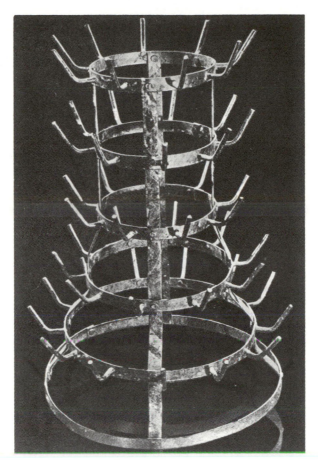

Figure 8-5. Marcel Duchamp, Bottlerack (original 1914, lost). Photograph is by Man Ray and is a part of Duchamp's Valise (1943), a collection of reproductions of Duchamp's art in a leather case (16⅛"h × 14¾"w × 4⅛"d). Collection, The Museum of Modern Art, New York. James Thrall Soby Fund.

Other artists have developed Duchamp's implicit criticism by creating conceptual art, in which a declared intention, the description of a project (often not feasible), or the performance of an act are the work of art. One example is described by Burnham (1973, p. 150):

Using a beach near his cottage at Truro, Massachusetts, [Douglas] Huebler decides to use the dimensions of a gallery in Los Angeles as boundaries for six sites on the beach. Markers are placed at six locations and Huebler makes photographs of each. These are assembled with a map and explanation and the piece is sent to the gallery in Los Angeles. The result on the gallery goer's part is a sense of double transposition.

a. The gallery in Los Angeles	b. The photos of the Truro beach with the gallery floor markers	c. The sites on Truro beach with markers the dimensions the gallery floor

These violations of the artist's freedom of choice (e.g., Martin's aleatory paintings), violations of persistence (e.g., Tinguely's self-destroying sculpture), violations of the need for elaborate technique (e.g., Duchamp's Readymades), and violations of the materiality of the work (e.g., Huebler's conceptual art), which test our very conception of the boundaries of art, are often characterized (by the many who find this art distasteful) as gimmicks, precisely because of the two ways in which they are like droodles: they are surprising when first encountered and their *visual* impact is unlikely to grow on future encounters. These works were created "not because they are 'good to see' but because they are 'good to think' " (Burnham, 1973, p. 46). Indeed, one might argue that the essence of the works in which Burnham sees historical transgressions is that they provide an insight into art or into our conception of art; they might be thought of as providing a *meta-aesthetic experience*. These works that hinge on a single insight, however penetrating, and that play the role of a single characterization, however apt, in an ongoing exploration of the scope and definition of art are likely to be branded as gimmicks because we expect meta-aesthetic experiences in the course of philosophical or critical discussions of art, not in art itself.[6]

In addition to the ephemerality of the experience afforded by perspective cabinets, there is another feature that suggests gimmickiness, namely, the reliance on a technological device, usually one that is relatively unfamiliar, and the emphasis of the technological device in attracting an audience to it. Sometimes the technology imposes unusual conditions on the viewer or listener, such as wearing special spectacles (for stereoscopic viewing), or earphones (for vivid stereophonic hearing), or requires very fine adjustment of complicated apparatus, such as an extraordinary sound-reproduction system. At least initially, such constraints and involvement with technology inspire complaints about gimmickry. Photography and film have suf-

---

[6] Rosenberg (1973) has made a very thorough analysis of these issues.

fered greatly from this technological stigma, for instance in Arnold Hauser's *The Social History of Art*:

The film is . . . an art evolved from the spiritual foundations of technics and, therefore, all the more in accordance with the medium in store for it. The machine is its origin, its medium and its most suitable subject. Films are "fabricated" and they remain tied to an apparatus, to a machine in a narrower sense than the products of the other arts. The machine here stands both between the creative subject and his work and between the receptive subject and his enjoyment of art. The motory, the mechanical, the automatically moving, is the basic phenomenon of the film. Running and racing, travelling and flying, escape and pursuit, the overcoming of spatial obstacles is the cinematic theme par excellence. . . . The film is above all a "photograph" and is already as such a technical art, with mechanical origins and aiming at mechanical repetition,[7] in other words, thanks to the cheapness of its reproduction, a popular and fundamentally "democratic" art. It is perfectly comprehensible that it suited bolshevism with its romanticism of the machine, its fetishism of technics, and its admiration for efficiency. Just as it is also comprehensible that the Russians and the Americans, as the two most technically-minded peoples, were partners and rivals in the development of this art. (1966, pp. 197–8)

Only in recent years have photography and film been recognized as forms of high art.[8]

Stereoscopic films are gimmicks not only because you must wear special spectacles to perceive the illusion, but also (and perhaps principally) because the stereoscopic films made to date were designed as showcases for the illusion (see Figure 8-6), replete with startling events such as objects hurtling at you and horrible, menacing monsters emerging from the screen to disembowel you. When such superficial application of the illusion fades out and is gradually replaced by an application that does not make the illusion the core of the experience, it ceases to be considered a

---

[7] Walter Benjamin, "L'Oeuvre d'art à l'époque de sa reproduction méchanisée," *Zeitschrift für Sozialforschung*, 1936, vol. 1, p. 45. [Hauser's footnote.]

[8] Even the use of so minimal a technological tool as a straight edge to produce straight lines in a painting is sometimes considered questionable. Could it be that the series of works by Albers called *Despite Straight Lines* is an ellipsis of the statement, "This is art, despite straight lines"?

Figure 8-6. Advertisement for a 3-D (stereoscopic) film

gimmick. Sergei Eisenstein thought stereoscopic films would come of age in this sense:

The stereoscopic film is the tomorrow of the cinema . . . [because] art "species" that survive are those whose structure accords with the innermost organic tendencies and requirements of both the creator and the spectator . . . [and] the three-dimensional principal in the stereoscopic film fully and consecutively answers some inner urge . . . it satisfies some inborn requirement of human nature. (1970, pp. 129–30)

We have noted three characteristics of illusion-producing devices that drive them out of the realm of art and evoke in us the impression that a gimmick is involved. First, some gimmicks are vulnerable to technical disclosure. Second, some gimmicks demand constrained conditions of observation. Third, gimmicks are accompanied by the sugges-

136

tion that the illusion is the principal experience to be had.

The peephole bears the latter two stamps of the gimmick: It requires the spectator to immobilize his or her eye at the peephole; and it is presented as a means of obtaining a powerful illusion of depth and thus focuses the observers' attention on the illusion rather than any other, more valuable aspects of the work.

The second reason Brunelleschi and his contemporaries had for abandoning the peephole method is more subtle than the avoidance of gimmicks and perhaps more important. After all, one should not exaggerate the difficulty of overcoming a public's prejudiced tendency to call a new technique a gimmick if it is put to varied and interesting uses. The second reason is related to the robustness of perspective. We have seen that the scene represented in a painting does not appear to undergo distortions when a spectator moves in front of it, and that the robustness of perspective implies that the spectator is able to infer the location of the center of projection of a perspective picture, to compensate for the projective distortion that the picture plane undergoes during the spectator's movement, and to see the picture as it would be seen from the center of projection. I have also hinted that the spectator experiences his or her body to be at this inferred center of projection and that this experience was intuitively discovered by the Renaissance painters and exploited in pictures that were designed so that they would never be seen from the center of projection (a phenomenon discussed in Chapter 6).

To convey how compellingly a painting puts you at its center of projection, we will analyze one of Mantegna's frescoes in the Ovetari Chapel. This painting produces this experience so effectively that it induced an eminent art historian into error. Frederick Hartt, in his *History of Italian Renaissance Art*, writes:

The lowest register of frescoes of the life of St. James begins just above the eye level of a person of average height for the Renaissance. The last two scenes, therefore, are planned as if Mantegna had a stage in front of him filled with models of human beings seeming to move downward as they recede from the eye. Thus only the feet of the figures nearest to the picture plane

Figure 8-7. Andrea Mantegna,
Saint James Led to Execution
(1454–7). Fresco. Ovetari Chapel,
Eremitani Church, Padua.

appear, in fact even break through the picture plane; the others
are cut off by the lower edge of the fresco. In the *St. James Led
to Execution* [Figure 8-7], we look up at the nearby buildings
portrayed with sharply real effect. . . . The coffering of the arched
gateway is also seen from below. But a moment's reflection will
disclose that if Mantegna had been consistent in his view, he
would have made the verticals converge as they rise, because
they are orthogonals leading to another vanishing point, high
above the scene. (1969, p. 350)

So strongly does Hartt feel that he is looking at the painting
from a low vantage point that he feels that his line of sight
must be tilted upward, which is equivalent to tilting the
image plane away from the vertical, which in turn implies
the convergence of vertical lines at a vanishing point.

But he is mistaken. A low center of projection does not
imply a tilted line of sight and image plane. To analyze
the experience provided by Mantegna's fresco, let us briefly
review the dilemma of perspective. Recall that some artists

138

placed their pictures so that they would not be seen from the center of projection (as Donatello did in *The Feast of Herod*, Figure 6-1). We have argued that, if the scene contains rectangular objects, the viewer will experience the picture as if it were viewed from the center of projection. Mantegna placed the center of projection at eye level but designed the picture so that the single vanishing point would be below the bottom of the frame. In this way, a viewer who looked at the painting would feel that the implicit vantage point (the perceived center of projection) is at the same *height* as the true vantage point. At the same time, if a viewer's gaze was directed at right angles to the picture plane along the implicit principal ray, the viewer would be focusing on a point *below the frame*. To further emphasize the strangeness of this projection, observe that *such a picture is hard to create by optical means*: Suppose you wanted to simulate the picture-taking process underlying this fresco using a standard camera. The only thing you could do would be to stage the scene on a platform somewhat above eye level and to hold the camera at eye level, pointing neither up nor down, "looking" at a point below the top of the platform. Because the developed picture would cover a vertical field more than double the field covered by Mantegna's, it would then be necessary to crop it just above the horizon line (see Figure 8-8).[9]

In other words, Mantegna has created a discrepancy much more subtle than Donatello's enforced disjunction of the viewer's vantage point from the center of projection: He allows the viewer to stand at the center of projection and then implies inconsistent directions for the observer's line of sight and for the principal ray of the central projection. The viewer's unconscious inference implies a principal ray

[9] This sort of "cropped perspective" is not unique: Vittore Carpaccio's *Arrival of the Ambassadors of Britain at the Court of Brittany* (ca. 1495) has its vanishing point to the left of the painting, and so the viewer feels that he or she is standing to the left of the Alberti window through which the scene is visible and is gazing toward that invisible vanishing point outside the painting. Carpaccio's painting is less disorienting than Mantegna's, possibly because our normal horizontal field of view is 37 degrees wide, whereas our normal vertical field of view is only 28 degrees high. See Chapter 7.

139

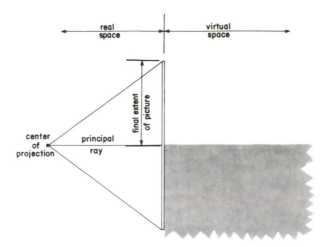

Figure 8-8. Explanation of central projection used in Mantegna's Saint James Led to Execution *(Figure 8-7)*

perpendicular to the image plane (in which case the viewer is looking at a wall), but the frame of the picture implies a visual axis at an oblique angle to the image plane (in which case the viewer is not looking at the horizon).

In Chapter 4, we discussed Leonardo's deep concern for the correspondence between the center of projection and the spectator's vantage point. To disregard this correspondence – he wrote – is tantamount to producing a perspective that would "look wrong, with every false relation and disagreement of proportion that can be imagined in a wretched work." And yet, as Leo Steinberg showed in a brilliant reexamination of the substance and form of Leonardo's *Last Supper*, Leonardo most blatantly – and successfully – violated his own rules.[10]

We first look at Pedretti's analysis of the perspective of the fresco (see Figures 8-9 and 8-10). The perspective construction of the fresco is not perfect: Different sets of orthogonals converge at different points.[11] The center of gravity of the triangle defined by three points is assumed

[10] The remainder of this chapter is heavily influenced by Steinberg (1973, Chapter IV). One of the most fascinating aspects of this monograph is Steinberg's study of replicas and adaptations of Leonardo's masterpiece by other painters. He makes an extremely strong case for presuming that whenever a replica or adaptation deviates from its model, the feature of the model that was not carried over is worth examining closely.

[11] The geometry of this badly damaged fresco may not be a faithful reflection of what it was when first painted.

Figure 8-9. Leonardo da Vinci, The Last Supper *(1495–8). Fresco. Church of Santa Maria delle Grazie, Milan.*

to be the vanishing point. Through the vanishing point the horizon line is drawn, labeled *L.O.* in Figure 8-10. The intersection of the present floor of the refectory with the picture plane is indicated by a line labeled *pavimento attuale*, and the level of the floor at Leonardo's time is marked by a line labeled *pavimento precedente*. The center of projection (which is at the height of the horizon) is 4.6 m (or 15 ft. 1 in.) above today's floor. The distance point (at the intersection of the diagonals of the ceiling coffering, assumed to be made up of square coffers), labeled *P.D.*, is 10.075 m (or 33 ft. 1 in.) from the vanishing point; therefore, the center of projection is 10.075 m, or between a quarter and a third of the length of the refectory away from the picture plane (Figure 8–11). At that distance, the picture's angular dimensions are 46 by 26 degrees. (To indicate a scale of angular measure, Pedretti has included a circle whose diameter subtends 60 degrees when viewed from the center of projection; it is labeled *cerchio visivo*.)

141

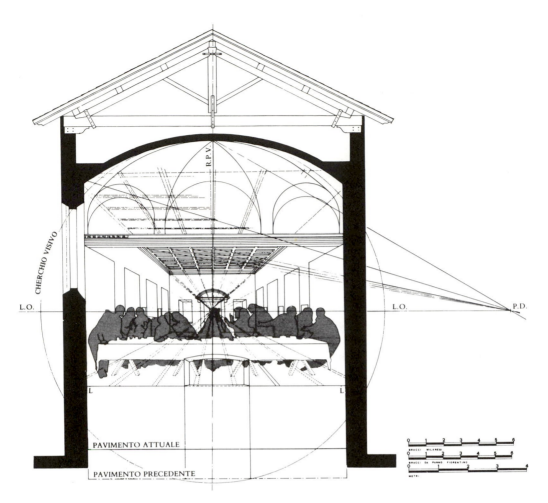

Figure 8-10. Analysis of perspective construction of Leonardo's Last Supper *superimposed on a cross section of refectory*

From Pedretti's analysis (which is very much in line with Steinberg's), we learn that, as Frederick Hartt put it, "there is no place in the refectory of Santa Maria delle Grazie where the spectator *can* stand to make the picture 'come right' " (1969, p. 401). The center of projection is so high that only a person about three times as tall as the average could see the picture from the center of projection.

But, from what I have explained in earlier chapters, a high center of projection should pose no problem: The robustness of perspective should take care of correcting for distortions caused by viewing the fresco from a vantage point that does not coincide with the center of projection. *The Last Supper* does, however, pose a problem, for Leonardo was not content to leave robust enough alone. He

142

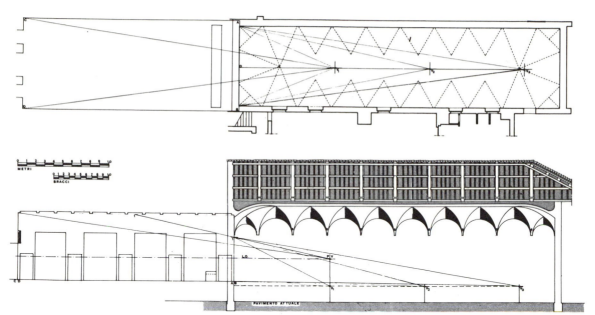

Figure 8-11. Reconstructed plan and longitudinal elevation of room represented in Leonardo's Last Supper, *in relation to plan and elevation of refectory*

did not just produce a space that is internally consistent; he created a space that suggests architectural continuity with the refectory, an illusionistic architecture along the lines we have discussed in Chapter 3. Unfortunately, no one has taken a photograph of the fresco from the center of projection. To get a feel for how well the fresco meshes with the line defined by the feet of the liernes that define the ten bays, consider the photograph shown in Figure 8-12, taken from approximately the height of the center of projection, somewhat too far to the left of the refectory, and about 25 m (roughly 82 ft.) too far.[12] The tops of the tapestries represented on the right wall of the room in which the Last Supper is taking place cry out to be aligned with the feet of the liernes on the side wall of the refectory. In Figure 8-13, which is a simulation of the view of the fresco from the height of the center of projection, and looking straight on at the vanishing point, but still somewhat too far away, the alignment of the feet of the liernes in the refectory with the tops of the tapestries in the fresco is quite close.

[12] Assuming the photographer stood between the seventh and eighth large bays away from the fresco.

143

Figure 8-12. Leonardo's Last Supper. *Photograph taken from a height of 4.5 m.*

Assuming that a viewer standing at the center of projection sees the virtual space in which the Last Supper takes place aligned with the real space of the refectory, we have an interesting problem. To judge from his writings, Leonardo seems at one point to have not believed in the robustness of perspective. As we saw in Chapter 4, he recommended that paintings be viewed from the center of projection or that the center of projection be "at least twenty times as far off as the greatest width or height of the objects represented" (Leonardo da Vinci, 1970, §544, pp. 325–6). In his *Last Supper*, he created a painting that no one, under normal circumstances, would see from the center of projection. Had he created a virtual space that did not suggest itself as an extension of the real space of the refectory, the robustness of perspective would have ensured that no distortions would be perceptible. But in addition to defining an elevated vantage point, he designed the architectural

144

Figure 8-13. Steinberg's cardboard model of the refectory with the line defined by the feet of the liernes drawn on the side walls

background of the *Last Supper* to mesh with the refectory in a way that could produce its illusionistic effect only when seen from the inaccessible center of projection. If this line of reasoning is correct, then this masterpiece further enriches the dialectical tension between the observer's station point and the center of projection of the painting. Because there is a suggestion of continuity between the real and the virtual architecture (very much as in Pozzo's ceiling), the inconsistency between them "pushes" you away from the low vantage point to which your body confines you, and "pulls" you up toward the center of projection, which resolves the tension. At the same time, the inconsistency helps you adopt a noncorrective way of looking at the fresco, one in which the you can pay attention to the rather jarring discrepancies between the virtual and real architecture. In this respect, Leonardo created a "difficult" work of art, one that forces you to engage in mental work to overcome the obstacles Leonardo has placed in your way to achieving an illusion of depth via perspective.

In fact, Leonardo did even more to make the work difficult. You will remember that Pedretti's measurements give a figure of 46 by 26 degrees for the angular extent of the fresco when seen from the center of projection. You will also recall that rectangular objects seen under an angle greater than 37 degrees are likely to appear distorted (Chapter 6). Nevertheless, none of the representations of right

145

angles (be they visible or implicit) violate Perkins's laws. And yet something is wrong. The shape of the virtual room represented in the fresco does not appear to be rectangular, but trapezoidal. To quote Steinberg:

> To one who can read a simple perspective, the suggestion that Leonardo's space is meant to be experienced as if on a trapezoidal plan comes as an affront – as though one didn't know how to read. The literate eye wants to interpret the waning width of the room as an illusion – not what is "really there." [We omit here an interesting footnote by Steinberg.] If the side walls seem bent on closing in behind Christ, our educated intelligence knows that such mere appearance must be discounted. (1973, p. 376)

Steinberg claims that this impression is caused by the failure of certain key features in the fresco (the upper edges of the hanging tapestries) to align with corresponding features in the refectory when the fresco is seen by a person standing on its floor. But even when the fresco is reproduced so that the walls of the refectory are invisible (Figure 8-9), that is, under conditions that allow the robustness of perspective to come into play, the impression of accelerated convergence remains. I believe that the impression is caused by Leonardo's unusual cropping of the upper part of the picture. If the ceiling had been allowed to extend to its intersection with the picture plane, I believe there would have been no tendency to perceive the plan of the virtual room as being trapezoidal. In the absence of such an uncropped picture, we can make a similar point by cropping the picture into conformity with more standard representations. In Figure 8-14, I have cropped the sides of the fresco. As a result, the impression of looking into a trapezoidal space is greatly diminished. The reason for the change is that, although none of the intersections that are part of the perspective construction violate Perkins's laws, the points at which the upper boundary of the picture intersects the ceiling–wall orthogonal is (to use the terminology introduced in Figure 6-17) a *tee*, and therefore cannot represent a rectangular corner. If, as we argued in Chapter 6, the presence of such local features affects our perception even though their component lines are not intended to be interpreted as belonging to one trihedral angle,

Figure 8-14. Cropped version of Leonardo's Last Supper

then the walls should have a tendency to be perceived as being in the same plane as the ceiling. Indeed, if one crops the bottom of the fresco, as in Figure 8-15, there is little to suggest that the light regions on either side of the coffered ceiling represent walls.

Was Leonardo aware of all these effects when he designed this painting? We shall never be certain. There is no question, as his notebook entry (quoted in Chapter 2) shows, that he was acutely aware of the problem of distortions caused by moving the eye away from the center of projection, and so it is extremely unlikely that any feature that we have discovered in this work escaped Leonardo's notice. Steinberg asked himself this question, and his answer serves us perfectly: "It is methodologically un-

147

Figure 8-15. Cropped version of Leonardo's Last Supper, *showing top part only*

sound to imagine Leonardo insensitive to the implications of his inventions" (1973, p. 369). There is one passage in Leonardo's late writings (Atlantic Codex, folio 111, v-b in the Ambrosian Library of Milan, written at least twenty years after he painted *The Last Supper*), that suggests that Leonardo may have understood the way in which perspective can induce an experience of elevation in the spectator:

And the figure painted when seen below from above will always appear as though seen below from above, *although the eye of the beholder may be lower than the picture itself.* (Emphasis supplied. Quoted by Pedretti, 1978, p. 39, footnote 1)

Let us recapitulate the lengthy argument of this chapter. We started with two general answers to the question why the Brunelleschi peephole was abandoned, namely, that peepholes are gimmicky and that, because of the robustness of perspective, peepholes are not necessary to achieve a compelling illusion of depth. In the latter part of this chapter, we discussed two masterpieces in which perspective was exploited to achieve effects that could not be achieved by any other means. Mantegna used perspective to produce a discrepancy between the direction of the spectator's gaze (upward) and the direction implicit in the orientation of the picture plane (horizontal). The result is a vibrantly tense work full of foreboding. Leonardo used perspective to elevate the viewer to an extraordinarily high center of projection, thus achieving a feeling of spiritual elevation. At the same time, the odd cropping of the top of the picture

148

tends to destroy the rectangularity of the room in which the Last Supper is taking place. As a result, there is an indefiniteness, an ambiguity, about the place, most befitting to the locale of an event so critical to the spiritual life of the church.

9

The psychology of egocenters

The fact that things overlap or are hidden does not enter into their definition, and expresses only my incomprehensible solidarity with one of them — my body.
Maurice Merleau-Ponty, from "Eye and mind"
(1964, p. 173)

I have mentioned several times the idea that, when we perceive a picture drawn in perspective from a vantage point other than the center of projection, our perceptual system infers the location of the center of projection and we feel that we are looking at the depicted scene from the vantage point implied by the center of projection. To explain the meaning of such a suggestion, I must first introduce the concept of *egocenter*. I will then discuss the question of a movable egocenter.

The notion of a spatially localized, visual egocenter that does not coincide with either eye is due to W. C. Wells (1792, cited by Ono, 1981), who was the first to devise a way of locating what came later to be called the "cyclopean eye." One simple method is this: Hold your head still while a friend stands a few feet away and points a stick at you. Have the friend change the position of the stick until you feel it pointing at you perfectly. Record the exact orientation of the stick. Now without moving your head ask your friend to stand somewhere else in the room, to the right or left of where he or she stood before, and adjust the orientation of the stick until it is pointing at you. If you do this several times, and you prolong the lines defined by the various positions of the stick when it is pointed at you, you will find that they all intersect approximately at one point inside your head just behind the midpoint of the line connecting your two eyes. This is the position of what is sometimes called the *sighting egocenter* (Howard, 1982, pp. 283–91).

In his philosophical essay "Where am I?", which may be the most amusing science-fiction story ever written, Daniel Dennett (1980) proposes a thought experiment: Imagine a surgical procedure that extirpates your brain from your head and connects radio transmitters to the stumps of the nerve cells that carry information from the brain to the rest of the body and radio receivers tuned to the same frequency on the complementary segments of these nerve cells in the body; similarly, this procedure connects radio transmitters to the stumps of the nerve cells that carry information from the body to the brain and appropriately tuned receivers of the sensory nerve cells in the brain. This is no more than, as one of the characters in Dennett's story puts it, "stretching the nerves."[1] After the operation, as soon as he is strong enough to be taken to see his brain, the hero of the story asks himself why he feels that he is outside the vat looking at his brain, rather than inside his brain being looked at by his eyes. After all, he argues, mental events are instantiated in the brain, so why does he not feel that he is where his mental events are instantiated? Although we should not take the "results" of Dennett's thought experiment, however plausible, too seriously, it is tempting to infer from them that the reason we feel that we are inside our heads or our bodies is not because all the important bodily or mental processes occur inside our body's skin; the experiment suggests that the spatial location of the machinery that makes mental events possible is irrelevant to our feeling of location. But if the location of the brain does not determine where we feel ourselves to be, what does? Perhaps it is the physical

---

[1] There is, to be sure, considerably more involved in performing such a technological feat, such as ensuring that the blood that flows through the extirpated brain has exactly the same composition as the blood coursing through the brainless body, because otherwise you could never get drunk, suffer from premenstrual tension, or become sexually aroused.

151

boundaries of our body that determine where we feel we are. Perhaps we feel that we are inside ourselves because our skin is where the outside ends. This simple answer can only be part of the truth. For where does our body end and the world begin? If you are walking in the dark feeling your way about with a cane, you are unaware of the pressure of the cane on the palm of your hand; all your attention is focused on the nature of the obstacles revealed by the tip of the cane. Under these circumstances, if you had to classify the cane as part of the world or part of your body, you would most likely say that it was part of your body. This is true of all tools. It is also true of vehicles. Most of the time when you drive an automobile, you are not aware of your points of contact with the inside of the automobile; it is as if you had grown a shell around you that you now inhabit and that your points of contact with the environment now coincide with the body of the automobile. Thus it is the external boundaries of your auto body and not the spaciousness of the car's interior that determine your feeling of how big a car you are in. In short, the boundary between the world and ourselves is extremely flexible.

Just how flexible this boundary is becomes clear when we consider the readiness with which we adopt virtual viewpoints in a movie theater. When the camera pans (see Figure 9-1), we feel ourselves turning to scan the environment; when the camera tilts, we feel ourselves tilting our heads to look upward or downward; when the camera engages in a tracking or traveling shot (e.g., when the camera is set on wheels or tracks), we feel ourselves traveling forward or backward with the camera. And yet we know all along that we are sitting in a movie theater.

In fact, as Michael Roemer clearly shows, the use of virtual points of view can make the difference between an effective but relatively shallow image and one that endures:

Audiences can be "played" by a skillful movie-maker with a fair amount of predictability, so that even discriminating audiences are easily taken in. At the beginning of Bergman's *Wild Strawberries* Professor Berg dreams that he is on a deserted street with all its doors and windows shuttered tight. He looks up at a clock that has no hands and pulls out his own watch only to find that its hands are missing also. A man appears on the corner with his head averted; when he turns, he has no face and his body dissolves into a pool on the sidewalk. A glass hearse comes down the street and spills a coffin that opens. Berg approaches and discovers his own body in the coffin. The corpse comes to life and tries to pull him in.

The nightmare quality in this sequence is derivative. The deserted, shuttered street, the clock and watch without hands, the glass hearse, the faceless man are all conventions familiar to surrealist painting and literature. Bergman uses them skillfully and with conviction to produce an effect in the audience, but they are not true film images, derived from life and rendered in concrete, physical terms.

There is a similar nightmare in Dreyer's *Vampire*. A young man dreams that he has entered a room with an open coffin in it. He approaches and discovers that he himself is the corpse. The camera now assumes the point-of-view of the dead man: we look up at the ceiling. Voices approach and two carpenters appear in our field of vision. They close the coffin with a lid but we continue to look out through a small glass window. Talking indistinctly, they nail down the lid and plane the edges of the

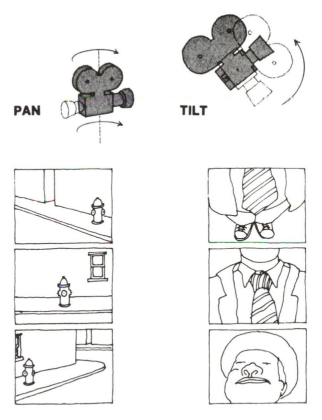

Figure 9-1. Definitions of two elementary camera movements: pan and tilt

153

wood. The shavings fall onto the window. One of them has put a candle down on the glass and wax drips onto it. Then the coffin is lifted up and we pass close under the ceiling, through the doorway, beneath the sunlit roofs and the church steeple of a small town – out into the open sky.

Here the detail is concrete: an experience is rendered, not cited; the situation is objective and out of it emerges, very powerfully, the feeling that Dreyer is after: a farewell to life, a last confined look at the earth before the coffin is lowered into the grave. (1966, pp. 259–60)

According to David N. Lee (Lee and Aronson, 1974; Lee and Lishman, 1975), the optic array (such as what we see in a movie theater) contains two sorts of information: information about the layout of objects in the environment, which is called *exteroceptive*[2] information, and information about the location of our body and its parts in the environment, which is called *exproprioceptive*[3] information. Although the exproprioceptive information we receive is usually consistent, in a movie theater we receive contradictory exproprioceptive information from two sources: Our eyes tell us that we are moving with the camera, while the pressure receptors in our skin tell us that we are sitting quietly in our seats. Whether we undergo both experiences at once or whether they alternate we do not know. It seems that in a movie theater our experiences are mostly due to the visual input; the visual source that tells us we are moving overrides the source that tells us we are sitting.

A similar type of visual dominance can be observed in the preservation of equilibrium, which is served by the semicircular canals in our inner ears, the sensors of pressure in our feet, and the visual sense. Without disturbing the semicircular canals or moving the feet, it is possible to cause a standing person to sway and on occasion to fall in an effort to compensate for the movement of the walls of a "swinging room" such as depicted in Figure 9-2.

Have someone trace a *b* or a *d* on your forehead and try to identify which of the two letters was traced. You will

---

[2] From the Latin *exterus* = exterior + *receptor* = receiver.
[3] From the Latin *ex* = out + *proprius* = one's own + *receptor* = receiver.

Figure 9-2. The moving room of Lee and Aronson (1974). It had three vertical sides and a ceiling, made of polystyrene foam stretched over a steel frame, but no floor. It was suspended so that it could swing noiselessly along an almost perfect horizontal path.

most likely feel somewhat uncomfortable carrying out this task, because you weren't told whose point of view to adopt: the writer's or your own. Now have the person trace one of these letters on the back of your head. You will probably not hesitate and report the letter as seen from behind your head. Now why is there some question regarding the correct point of view to adopt when a letter is traced on your forehead and no question regarding which point of view to adopt when the letter is traced on the back of your head? After all, if you are "reading" the letter from within your head, the same ambiguity should arise when the letter is written on the back of your head: to read from within looking backward or to read from outside looking forward. There is one way of making sense of this dilemma: Suppose we do not mind moving our vantage point in or out of our heads, but we try to avoid two things: turning our vantage point backward and "reading" through the skull. In the case of writing on the forehead, we cannot avoid doing one of the things we wish to avoid; in the case of writing on the back of the head, we can simply move our vantage point behind the head and "read" the letter from there.

To find out why we resist turning our vantage point backward compared to our avoidance of reading through the skull, we must refine our technique somewhat. Instead of simply asking people to report which letter was traced on the head, we can assign a vantage point to them and tell them to adopt one of four vantage points.

Rear vantage point. Wherever a letter is traced on the head, it should be interpreted from a vantage point behind the head looking forward. If the letter is traced on the forehead, it should be read as if the head were transparent and the letter was written in opaque ink.

Front vantage point. Wherever a letter is traced on the head, it should be interpreted from a vantage point in front of the head looking backward. Letters traced on the back of the head should be read as if the head were transparent.

Internal vantage point. Wherever a letter is traced on the head, it should be interpreted from a vantage point inside the head looking radially outward through the transparent skull. Thus the vantage point faces forward to read a letter traced on the forehead and backward to read a letter traced on the back of the head.

External vantage point. Wherever a letter is traced on the head, it should be interpreted from a vantage point outside the head looking radially inward at the skull. Thus the vantage point faces forward to read a letter traced on the back of the head and backward to read a letter traced on the forehead.

Now suppose we measured the amount of time it took to read letters traced on the forehead and on the back of

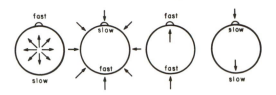

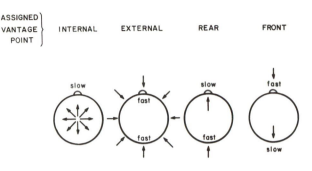

Figure 9-3. Predictions for speed of "reading" letters traced on the head for four assigned vantage points. Top panel: under assumption that reading is mostly hindered by turning vantage point backward. *Bottom panel:* under assumption that reading is mostly hindered by having to read through skull.

the head for each of the four vantage points. We could then find out whether the correct interpretation of the traced letter is slowed down more by having to read through the skull or by having to turn one's vantage point (see Figure 9-3). To clarify this figure, let us discuss the predictions for the rear and front vantage points under the two hypotheses. If of the two obstacles to reading, turning the vantage point is a greater hindrance than reading through the skull, then the letters should be read rapidly regardless of whether they are traced on the forehead or the back of the head; if, on the other hand, reading through the skull is the greater obstacle, then letters traced on the back of the head should be read more quickly than letters traced on the forehead. Considering now the front vantage point, if facing backward is a greater hindrance than reading through the skull, then the letters should be read slowly wherever they are traced; if, on the other hand, reading through the skull is the difficulty, then letters traced on the forehead should be read more quickly than those traced on the back of the head. Similarly, this reasoning applies to the remaining two vantage points.

In an experiment begun with Janice Marcus (a graduate student at Yale) and concluded with David Turock and Thomas Best (graduate students at Rutgers) (Kubovy et

157

al., unpub.), instead of having letters traced on just one position on the forehead and one position on the back of the head, there were eight positions, three of which we consider to be forehead positions and three of which we consider to be on the back of the head. The results were unequivocal in their support for our first hypothesis, namely, that it is harder for us to turn our vantage point than to read through the skull.

If turning the vantage point is difficult and seeing through the skull is easy, then there is a hypothesis that can account for all our data, which we call the *disembodied-eye hypothesis*. Suppose that patterns traced on the skin are interpreted as if they were read by a disembodied eye that has a preferred position behind the head looking forward. It would take us too far afield to discuss the pros and cons of this hypothesis; suffice it to say that, although it has some drawbacks, this hypothesis has served us well as an aid to thinking about the perception of patterns traced on the skin and has not been successfully challenged by any alternative. The main attraction of the hypothesis in the context of the present analysis of perspective is that it gives some content to the idea of projecting one's egocenter to locations in space outside one's body. Furthermore, the fact that subjects in our experiments are able to adopt a variety of vantage points when instructed to do so suggests that the egocenter (or disembodied eye) is flexible and need not remain in one position. We are still far from a true understanding of this fascinating problem of vantage points in art and in perception in general, but, given the sorts of evidence we now have, the notion of a movable egocenter cannot be treated any more as a frivolous fancy.

We have reached the point where the fifth purpose of perspective, mentioned in the introduction, can be summarized. I claim that, for viewers familiar with perspective, powerful effects can be achieved by creating discrepancies between the natural direction of the viewer's line of sight and the line of sight implicit in the perspective of the painting (as was the case with Mantegna's *Saint James Led to Execution*, Figure 8-7), or by locating the center of projection high above the viewer's eye level (as in Leonardo's

Last Supper, Figure 8-9). These effects achieve the goal of divorcing the viewer's felt point of view in relation to the scene represented in the painting from the viewer's felt position in relation to the room in which he or she is standing. We cannot do more, in our present state of knowledge, than to speculate on the effect of such discrepancies, which I believe induce a feeling of spirituality, perhaps one conducive to a religious experience: a separation of the mind's eye from the bodily eye. Such effects were very much in accord with the aims of the Renaissance painters, who wished to convey a religious experience through their art. For, as Paul Oskar Kristeller points out in his discussion of paganism and Christianity in Renaissance thought,

if an age where the nonreligious concerns that had been growing for centuries attained a kind of equilibrium with religious and theological thought, or even began to surpass it in vitality and appeal, must be called pagan, the Renaissance was pagan, at least in certain places and phases. Yet since the religious convictions of Christianity were either retained or transformed, but never really challenged, it seems more appropriate to call the Renaissance a fundamentally Christian age. (1961, p. 73)

Furthermore, the divorce of the mind's eye from the bodily eye is very much in the spirit of Renaissance Platonism. Plato's thought and Neoplatonism, which had been eclipsed during medieval times, were revived by Marsilio Ficino (see Introduction). Kristeller writes as follows about Ficino's theory of contemplation:

In the face of ordinary daily experiences, the mind finds itself in a state of continuous unrest and dissatisfaction, but it is capable of turning away from the body and the external world and of concentrating upon its own inner substance. (1967, p. 198)

Now I do not mean to equate Ficino's concept of contemplation with the use of perspective to separate the mind's eye from the bodily eye. Nevertheless, I do wish to suggest that such a use of perspective is in keeping with the spiritual concerns of intellectuals in the late fifteenth and early sixteenth centuries.

The lack of contemporary analyses of this issue is per-

Figure 9-4. The Parthenon, from northwest (447–432 B.C.)

Figure 9-5. Diagram in exaggerated proportion of horizontal curvature of Parthenon

haps puzzling at first blush. However, when we recall how little was written about perspective in general during the fifteenth and early sixteenth centuries, one's surprise wanes somewhat. Furthermore, when we look back at the ground we have covered up to this point in this book, it becomes apparent that our understanding of optics, geometry, and perception is far more advanced than it was half a millennium ago. It is not surprising, therefore, that Renaissance artists had to proceed more by intuition and rule of thumb than by analysis and deduction; whatever discoveries they made were most likely in the form of tacit knowledge, which is notoriously difficult to understand and analyze. Furthermore, this is not the only time in the history of art that subtle and complex procedures were developed to achieve perceptual and spiritual effects, for which little or no documentary evidence remains, the Parthenon (see Figure 9-4) being a prime example. Just as the Renaissance artists deviated from the geometric dictates of perspective, the Parthenon deviates from mathematical regularity in several ways. One of these is illustrated in Figure 9-5. To this very day, several theories concerning the purpose of these so-called refinements compete for the favor of scholars (Carpenter, 1970; Pollitt, 1972).

10 The invention of perspective and the evolution of art

> *...the jury wrote down all three dates on their slates and then added them up, and reduced the answer to shillings and pence.*
> Lewis Carroll, from "Alice's Adventures in Wonderland," 1865 (Carroll, 1976, p. 117)

In this last chapter, I will discuss three views of the place of perspective in the history of art: those of Panofsky, Goodman, and Gablik. The first two are relativists and claim that perspective is a convention of representation adopted during the Renaissance. Gablik has proposed an interesting parallel between the development of cognitive abilities in children and the evolution of art.

In his book on *The Renaissance Rediscovery of Linear Perspective*, Samuel Edgerton wrote a masterly exposition of Panofsky's seminal article "Die Perspektive als 'symbolische Form' " (Panofsky, 1924/25) and of its reception among scholars interested in perspective. I will quote extensively from his discussion because it serves so well to introduce the points I wish to make in conclusion.

This article created extraordinary interest in subsequent decades [after its publication in 1927] because the author argued that linear perspective by no means conclusively defined visual reality, rather that it was only a particular constructional approach for representing pictorial space, one which happened to be peculiar to the culture of the Italian Renaissance.

Art historians, trying at that time to justify the rise and spread of modern abstract art, were pleased because Panofsky seemed to be saying that linear perspective was not the last word in pictorial truth, that it, too, could pass away as had all earlier artistic conventions... Such a notion has since been expressly defended by various writers on art and psychology, among them Rudolph Arnheim [1974], Gyorgy Kepes [1944], and Nelson Goodman [1976, as well as Francastel, 1951, and Suzi Gablik, 1976].

However, Panofsky's essay did contain one egregious error. With ingenious reasoning, the author tried to show that the ancient Greeks and Romans – Euclid and Vitruvius in particular – conceived of the visual world as curved, and that since the retina is in fact a concave surface, we do indeed tend to see straight lines as curved. . . .

Panofsky's essay, particularly in recent years, has come under criticism from scientists, as well as from E. H. Gombrich [1969, 1976, 1980] and other scientific-minded art historians. Writers on optics and perceptual psychology such as James J. Gibson [1971], G. ten Doesschate [1964], and M. H. Pirenne [1952–3] have challenged Panofsky for his subjective curvature hypothesis and denial that linear perspective has a catholic or "ultimate" veracity. They are especially put off by Panofsky's reference to perspective as a "symbolic form," which is to say, a mere convention . . . Unfortunately, Panofsky never explained definitively just what he meant by the phrase "symbolic form." However, he certainly has in mind a more subtle meaning than a "system of conventions [like][1] versification in poetry." [This is how Pirenne summarized Panofsky's theory.] Indeed, Professor Pirenne and other scientist critics misunderstand the ingenuity of Panofsky's approach as much as they find Panofsky himself misunderstood classical optics and modern perceptual psychology. (1975, pp. 153–5)

Edgerton proceeds to show how Panofsky's notion of symbolic form is inspired by Ernst Cassirer's Kantian philosophy, which he capsulates as follows:

The symbols man uses to communicate ideas about the objective world have an autonomy all their own. Indeed, the human mind systematizes these symbols into structures that develop quite independently of whatever order might exist in the natural world to begin with . . .

The real thrust of [Panofsky's] essay was not to prove that the ancients believed the visual world was curved or that Renaissance perspective was a mere artistic convention, but that *each historical period in Western civilization had its own special "perspective,"* a particular symbolic form reflecting a particular *Weltanschauung*. Thus linear perspective was the peculiar answer of the Renaissance period to the problem of representing space . . .

---

[1] Edgerton's interpolation.

In the 15th century, there emerged mathematically ordered "systematic space," infinite, homogeneous, and isotropic, making possible the advent of linear perspective . . . Linear perspective, whether "truth" or not, thus became the symbolic form of the Italian Renaissance because it reflected the general world view of the Italian people at this particular moment in history. (1975, pp. 156, 157–8)

As Edgerton so well explains, Panofsky's position was not blithely relativistic: It is more important to understand why the artists of the Renaissance were interested in perspective than to determine whether it is the "correct" method of representation. In this book, I have attempted to convey the variety as well as subtlety of the reasons why Renaissance artists were interested in perspective. I hope I have persuaded the reader that "truth" was not at stake here. To be sure, perspective was a system that enabled artists to represent space according to geometric rules. Mainly, however, it was a framework within which originality without arbitrariness[2] could be achieved.

Nelson Goodman took the issue a step further by marshaling all his philosophical arguments in support of the relativistic conception of perspective. Goodman's sustained analysis of the notions of representation, realism, and resemblance is also an impassioned defense of the argument that perspective is not an absolute standard of fidelity, that it is but one of many methods of representation. According to Goodman, depictions are analogous to descriptions, and descriptions need not resemble the things they describe. Indeed, sometimes they cannot resemble the thing they are describing because that thing simply doesn't exist (e.g., a unicorn). Why then do we think that a picture should resemble the thing it represents? Goodman answers that conventions of representation are responsible for this misapprehension. From the correct observation that a picture usually resembles *other* pictures of the same kind of thing, we tend to infer that a picture resembles the kind of thing it represents. The key argument is here: Goodman asks himself whether

[2] The term is Wimsatt's (1968, p. 80).

164

the most realistic picture is the one that provides the greatest amount of pertinent information. But this hypothesis can be quickly and completely refuted. Consider a realistic picture, painted in ordinary perspective and normal color, and a second picture just like the first except that the perspective is reversed and each color is replaced by its complementary. The second picture, appropriately interpreted, yields exactly the same information as the first. . . . The alert absolutist will argue that for the second picture but not the first we need a key. Rather, the difference is that for the first the key is already at hand. For proper reading of the second picture, we have to discover rules of interpretation and apply them deliberately. Reading of the first is by virtually automatic habit; practice has rendered the symbols so transparent that we are not aware of any effort, of any alternatives, or of making any interpretation at all. (1976, pp. 35–6)

I believe that I have provided us with the tools to refute Goodman's radical relativism.[3] I have shown that perspective is not a thoroughgoing, arbitrary application of the geometric system of central projection. Rather, it is a geometric system tempered by what perception can or cannot do. It has evolved into a system adapted to the capabilities of our perceptual system. To respond, Goodman would have to claim that what perception can do depends on what it learned to do, and that there is no limit to what perception can learn. But that argument is false. There are clear limits to the extent of perceptual rearrangement (induced by wearing prisms, mirrors, and other devices that modify the form of the optical information reaching our eyes) to which human beings can adapt. We cannot arbitrarily change the way we perceive optical information, nor can we arbitrarily change our motor responses to it, regardless of the amount of time or effort we might invest in doing so (Welch, 1978, pp. 277–9).

We have seen that Panofsky's view on the conventionality of perspective may not have been as extreme as some have interpreted it to be because it does not exaggerate the importance of the role played by the "correct" representation of space in Renaissance art. We have also seen that

---

[3] See also Gombrich's (1982) broader attack on Goodman's conventionalistic position.

Goodman's view, on the other hand, is the most radical position on this matter that one can take precisely because it makes the "correctness" of perspective into a central issue, thereby impoverishing our understanding of perspective in Renaissance art rather than enriching it. We turn now to a third view, which shares some of the features of Goodman's approach. Suzi Gablik, in her book *Progress in Art*, has presented a cultural analog of the classical embryological law, "ontogeny recapitulates phylogeny," according to which an embryo, in the course of its maturation, goes through stages during which it takes on the appearances of its evolutionary ancestors. Gablik has proposed a similar law for the evolution of art, which I call "sophogeny recapitulates ontogeny," namely, that the evolution of cultural wisdom parallels the development of the individual. I will argue that Gablik, to make her point, emphasizes only one of the goals of Renaissance perspective – the representation of objects in space – and that she implies that art cannot achieve this goal without being rigid and inflexible, rule-bound and lacking in true conceptual autonomy.

Gablik's point of departure is the theory of cognitive development of Jean Piaget, the celebrated Swiss psychologist. Piaget proposed that it is possible to discover milestones in the development of thinking, perception, problem solving, and all the other cognitive abilities. He distinguished three major stages in cognitive development. In *the preoperational stage* (which ends at about 5 years of age), children have a very poor grasp of causality and reversibility. For instance, if you pour a liquid from a tall, narrow glass to fill a squat, short one of equal capacity, refill the tall glass with liquid, and then ask a preoperational child which glass contains more liquid, the child will say that the taller glass contains more. The child does not understand the concepts of *conservation* (of the amount of fluid) and of *compensation* (the trade-off of height for area of the cross section), which are physical expressions of the formal concept of reversibility. In the *concrete-operational stage* (which runs to about the age of 10), children understand the reversibility underlying certain physical opera-

166

Table 10-1. *Stages of cognitive development and megaperiods of art history.*

Stages of cognitive development	Spatial characteristics	Megaperiods of art history
ENACTIVE MODE		
Preoperational stage: The stage at which representations are characterized by static imagery and space is subjectively organized. Psychical and physical ideas are not yet dissociated.	*Topological relations:* Distance between objects is based on their proximity to one another on a two-dimensional plane which only takes height and breadth into account. Absence of depth, no unified global space which conserves size and distance.	*Ancient and Medieval* (including Graeco-Byzantine, ancient Oriental, Egyptian, archaic Greek, and early medieval)
ICONIC MODE		
Concrete-operational stage: The stage at which representation can arrange all spatial figures in coordinate systems. Representation is still attached to its perceptual content, however. The emergence of perspective as a formal logic, applicable to any content whatsoever, but still confined to empirical reality and to the concrete features of the perceptual world.	*Projective and Euclidean relations:* Based on the static viewpoint of a single observer. Separation of observer and world.	*The Renaissance*
SYMBOLIC MODE		
Formal-operational stage: The stage at which hypothetical-deductive, logico-mathematical, and propositional systems emerge, constructed and manipulated as independent relational entities without reference to empirical reality.	*Indeterminate, atmospheric space* (late Monet, Cubism, Rothko): Space as an all-over extension in which all points are of equal status and are relative to each other. No dominance of volume over void. (Pollock)	*The Modern period* (including late Impressionism, Cubism, Formalism, Serial art, art governed by logical systems and by propositional thinking)

Source: Gablik, 1976, p. 43.

tions but are unable to deal with the logical concepts that are their abstract representation. Finally, in the *formal-operational stage*, children can understand abstract logical and mathematical structures that underly reality.

At this point, we should let Gablik speak for herself:

According to our own cognitive map [Table 10-1] . . . it would seem that a fully developed formal-operational stage has not appeared in the art of any culture except that of post-Renaissance Western art. . . . Now if defining the history of art in terms of

167

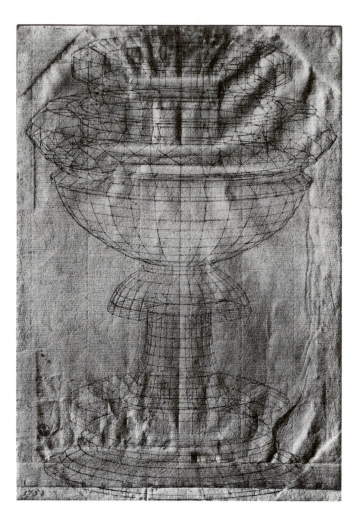

Figure 10-1. Paolo Uccello, Perspective Study of a Chalice (1430–40). Pen and ink. Gabinetto dei Disegni e Stampe, Florence.

cognitive stages is of any value, it is to the extent that it may contribute to explaining the importance of this development – specifically, of an increase in the autonomy of forms to the point where even abstract forms devoid of content can be constructed and manipulated. (Compare, in this regard, Uccello's drawing of a chalice [Figure 10-1] with Sol LeWitt's open modular cubes [Figure 10-2], or Leonardo's *War Machine* [Figure 10-3] with Malevich's *Suprematist Elements* [Figure 10-4].)[4] . . . In making the seemingly paradoxical assertion that these contemporary works, which when viewed on their own appear to be visually

---

[4] I suppose that Gablik wants us to compare the two squares and the circle in the Malevich to the divided box and the wheel in the Leonardo. There is something odd in this comparison: We are being asked to compare two juxtaposed paintings by Malevich to one drawing by Leonardo. I fail to see how such a comparison can possibly be meaningful.

168

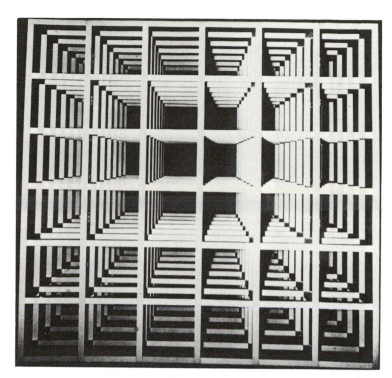

Figure 10-2. Sol LeWitt, untitled (1969). Baked enamel and aluminum. John Weber Gallery, New York.

much simpler than a Renaissance painting, are in reality *more complex*, I refer to the complexity which is occasioned by the Modern paradigm viewed as a whole, and to the infinite number of systems which it is able to generate. The Renaissance paradigm derives from a single, closed logical system – perspective – which is repeated over and over again in every picture in much the same way, so that every picture is rigidly bound and dictated by the rules of the system. The Modern paradigm is characterized by its openness and by the infinite number of possibilities and positions which can be taken. (1976, pp. 44–5)

Gablik can make her case only if she can demonstrate that Renaissance artists used perspective rigidly and concretely:

The belief that the universe is ordered and rationally explicable in terms of geometry was part of a deterministic world-picture which viewed nature as stable and unchanging, and considered that mastery of it could be achieved by universal mathematical principles. The spatial illusionism of one-point perspective re-flected a world which was permanent and fixed in its ways, modelled on an absolute space and time unrelated to any outward circumstance. One has only to look at [paintings by] Piero della Francesca [see Figure 10-5] or . . . Bellini [see Figure 10-6] to sense this immutability of things: a world is portrayed in which

169

Figure 10-3. *Leonardo da Vinci,* A War Machine *(Codex Atlanticus, Folio 387ʳ). Drawing.*

Figure 10-4. *Kasimir Malevich:*
Left: Suprematist Elements: Two Squares *(1913). Pencil. Sheet: 19¾ × 14¼". Composition: 6¾ × 11¼". Collection, The Museum of Modern Art, New York.*
Right: Suprematist Element: Circle *(1913). Pencil. Sheet: 18½ × 14⅜". Composition: 11½ × 11⅛". Collection, The Museum of Modern Art, New York.*

chance and indeterminacy play no part. From this vantage point, we can see how a totally mathematized philosophy of nature was the dominant influence on the course of Western painting, and how these processes of mathematics offer themselves as a bridge from one stage in the development of art to the next.

In the Renaissance, geometry was truth and all nature was a vast geometrical system. (The book of nature, Galileo wrote, is written in geometrical characters.) Perspective images were based on observation, but they were rationalized and structured by

Figure 10-5. Piero della Francesca (attrib. doubtful), Perspective of an Ideal City (ca. 1470). Panel. Galleria Nazionale delle Marche, Palazzo Ducale, Urbino.

mathematics. For Alberti in 1435, the first requirement of a painter was to know geometry; and Piero, in *De Prospettiva Pingendi*, virtually identified painting with perspective, writing three treatises to show how the visible world could be reduced to mathematical order by the principles of perspective and solid geometry. (1976, p. 70)

These views stress the rigidity, the rationality, and the immutability of the laws of perspective. Undoubtedly, there is some truth in Gablik's portrait of an era fascinated by geometry. But fascination is not fetishism. During the Renaissance, geometry was always subordinate to perception: I have shown how the geometry of central projection was routinely violated to counteract its perceptually unacceptable effects. We have seen that perspective was far from being a single, closed, logical system that was repeated over and over. Gablik has produced a caricature of Renaissance art, which even with regard to its use of perspective was far from being rigid and uncompromising. To be sure, perspective was used for a representational purpose, and in that respect it remained tied to the concrete objects it served to represent. But it also served to explore other aspects of experience. Indeed, it is possible to make a case against Gablik's position by applying a slightly different set of Piagetian concepts. Taking my analysis of the effects of perspective as a point of departure, one might argue that the Renaissance artists were exploring the nature of egocentrism and ways of using perspective to *free* oneself from one's special vantage point. To do so is a sign of one's ability to transcend egocentrism. One might argue that the Cubists were engaged in a similar exploration, but can one say that they were, in this respect, more advanced

171

Figure 10-6. Gentile Bellini,
Procession of the Relic of the
True Cross *(1496). Canvas. Acca-*
demia, Venice.

than were the Renaissance artists? And certainly one would
not claim that Sol LeWitt's sculpture is part of such an
investigation. I am convinced that by carefully selecting
the dimensions along which comparisons between different periods of art were made, one could develop an argument that *any* period in art is more advanced than all
the others.[5]

We have disagreed with Goodman; perspective is not
mere convention. We have disagreed with Gablik; sophogeny does not recapitulate ontogeny. And Panofsky was
mistaken on some matters. But Panofsky had an extremely
useful formulation of the importance of perspective: It
served as symbolic form. Even though perspective has a
very sturdy geometric and perceptual foundation, which
makes it, in some sense, the best method to represent space
on a flat surface, the question of whether perspective is
"true" is far less important than the inquiry about how

[5] A similar thesis was presented by Gowans (1979), apparently formulated
without knowledge of Gablik's book. As one who disagrees with this
theory, I find some satisfaction in noting a 700-year discrepancy between
their chronologies. According to Gowans, the Piagetian stage of formal
operations was attained by the Romanesque period (twelfth century),
whereas according to Gablik it wasn't attained until late Impressionism
(late nineteenth century).

perspective was put to use by Renaissance artists in an artistic context. I have tried to answer this question and to show that these uses were far removed from the oversimplified view of perspective as a procrustean system in the service of crass illusionism. Perspective often enabled the Renaissance artist to cast the deeply religious contents of his art in a form that could produce in the viewer spiritual effects that could not have been achieved by any other formal means. In that sense, perspective should be viewed as "symbolic form."

References

Adams, K. R. Perspective and the viewpoint. *Leonardo*, 1972, 5, 209–17.

Alberti, L. B. *Ten books on architecture*. London: Alec Tiranti, 1955. First pub. 1485. This translation first published 1755.

Alberti, L. B. *On painting*. Ed. J. R. Spencer. New Haven, Conn.: Yale University Press, 1966. First pub. 1435–6.

Anstis, S. M., Mayhew, J. W., and Morley, T. The perception of where a face or television 'portrait' is looking. *American Journal of Psychology*, 1969, *82*, 474–89.

Arcangeli, F. Un nodo problematico nei rapporti fra Leon Battista Alberti e il Mantegna. In *Il Sant' Andrea di Mantova e Leon Battista Alberti*. Mantua: Biblioteca Communale, 1974.

Arnheim, R. *Art and visual perception: A psychology of the creative eye; the new version*. Berkeley: University of California Press, 1974.

Arnheim, R. Brunelleschi's peepshow. *Zeitschrift für Kunstgeschichte*, 1978, *41*, 57–60.

Attneave, F. Apparent movement and the what–where connection. *Psychologia*, 1974, *17*, 108–20.

Baird, J. C. The moon illusion: II. A reference theory. *Journal of Experimental Psychology: General*, 1982, *111*, 304–15.

Baird, J. C., and Wagner, M. The moon illusion: I. How high is the sky? *Journal of Experimental Psychology: General*, 1982, *111*, 296–303.

Battisti, E. Note sulla prospettiva rinascimentale. *Arte Lombarda*, 1971, *16*, 87–97.

Bradley, D. R., Dumais, S. T., and Petry, H. M. Reply to Cavonius. *Nature*, May 6, 1976, *261*, 77–8.

Burnham, J. *The structure of art*. New York: Braziller, 1973. Rev. ed.

Cage, J. *Silence: lectures and writings*. Middletown, Conn.: Wesleyan University Press, 1973.

Carpenter, R. *The architects of the Parthenon*. Harmondsworth, England: Penguin Books, 1970.

Carrà, C. La peinture des sons, bruits et odeurs. Manifeste Futuriste.

1913. In collection of Beineke Rare Book and Manuscript Library, Yale University.

Carroll, L. *The complete works of Lewis Carroll*. New York: Vintage Books, 1976.

Coleridge, S. T. *Biographia literaria*. Ed. J. Shawcross. Oxford: Clarendon Press, 1907.

Cooper, B. Development of sensitivity to geometric information for viewing shapes and sizes in pictures. In R. N. Haber (ed.), *Proceedings of the Tenth Symposium of the Center for Visual Sciences*. Rochester: University of Rochester, 1977.

Danto, A. C. *The transfiguration of the commonplace: a philosophy of art*. Cambridge, Mass.: Harvard University Press, 1981.

Dars, C. *Images of deception: the art of trompe-l'oeil*. Oxford: Phaidon, 1979.

Dennet, D. Where am I? In *Brainstorms*. Cambridge, Mass.: MIT Press, 1980.

De Santillana, G. The role of art in the scientific renaissance. In M. Clagett (ed.), *Critical problems in the history of science*. Madison: University of Wisconsin Press, 1959.

Descargues, P. *Perspective*. New York: Abrams, 1977.

Doesschate, G. ten. *Perspective: fundamentals, controversials, history*. Nieuwkoop, The Netherlands: B. de Graaf, 1964.

Draper, S. W. *Reasoning about depth in line-drawing interpretation*. Doctoral dissertation, University of Sussex, 1980.

Edgerton, S. Y., Jr. *The Renaissance rediscovery of linear perspective*. New York: Basic Books, 1975.

Eisenstein, S. *Notes of a film director*. New York: Dover, 1970. First pub. in Russian after 1948.

Eliot, T. S. *Collected poems*. London: Faber and Faber, 1963.

Farber, J., and Rosinski, R. R. Geometric transformation of pictured space. *Perception*, 1978, *1*, 269–82.

Filarete (Antonio de Piero Averlino). *Treatise on architecture*. Ed. J. R. Spencer. New Haven, Conn.: Yale University Press, 1965. Written between 1461 and 1464.

Finke, R. A., and Kurtzman, H. S. Mapping the visual field in mental imagery. *Journal of Experimental Psychology: General*, 1981, *110*, 501–17.

Francastel, P. *Peinture et société: naissance et destruction d'un espace plastique de la Renaissance au Cubisme*. Paris: Audin, 1951.

Frommel, C. L. *Die Farnesina und Peruzzis architektonisches Frühwerk*. Berlin: Walter de Gruyter, 1961.

Gablik, S. *Progress in art*. London: Thames and Hudson, 1976.

Gadol, J. *Leon Battista Alberti: universal man of the early Renaissance*. Chicago: University of Chicago Press, 1969.

Gibson, J. J. A theory of pictorial perception. *Audio-visual Communication Review*, 1954, *1*, 1–23.

175

Gibson, J. J. The information available in pictures. *Leonardo*, 1971, *4*, 27–35.

Gibson, J. J. *The ecological approach to visual perception*. Boston: Houghton Mifflin, 1979.

Gill, R. W. *Basic perspective*. London: Thames and Hudson, 1974.

Gill, R. W. *Creative perspective*. London: Thames and Hudson, 1975.

Gioseffi, J. J. Perspective. In *Encyclopedia of world art*. New York: McGraw-Hill, 1966.

Girgus, J. J., Rock, I., and Egatz, R. The effect of knowledge of reversibility on the reversibility of ambiguous figures. *Perception and Psychophysics*, 1977, *22*, 550–6.

Goffman, E. *Frame analysis: An essay on the organization of experience*. Cambridge, Mass.: Harvard University Press, 1974.

Goldstein, E. B. Rotation of objects in pictures viewed at an angle: evidence for different properties of two types of pictorial space. *Journal of Experimental Psychology: Human Perception and Performance*, 1979, *5*, 78–87.

Gombrich, E. H. *Meditations on a hobby horse*. London: Phaidon, 1963.

Gombrich, E. H. *Art and illusion: a study in the psychology of pictorial representation*. Princeton, N.J.: Princeton University Press, 1969. 2d ed.

Gombrich, E. H. Illusion and art. In R. L. Gregory and E.H. Gombrich (eds.), *Illusion in nature and art*. New York: Scribner, 1973.

Gombrich, E. H. *Means and ends: Reflections on the history of fresco painting*. London: Thames and Hudson, 1976.

Gombrich, E. H. Standards of truth: the arrested image and the moving eye. In W. J. T. Mitchell (ed.), *The language of images*. Chicago: University of Chicago Press, 1980. Reprinted in *Critical Inquiry*, 1980, *7*, 237–73, and in E. H. Gombrich, *The image and the eye: further studies in the psychology of pictorial representation*. Ithaca, N.Y.: Cornell University Press, 1982.

Gombrich, E. H. Image and code: scope and limits of conventionalism in pictorial representation. In *The image and the eye: further studies in the psychology of pictorial representation*. Ithaca, N.Y.: Cornell University Press, 1982.

Goodman, N. *Languages of art: an approach to a theory of symbols*. Indianapolis: Hackett, 1976. 2d ed.

Gowans, A. Child art as an instrument for studying history: the case for an "ontogeny repeats phylogeny" paradigm in universal history. *Art History*, 1979, *2*, 247–74.

Graves, R. *Collected poems*. Garden City, N.Y.: Anchor Books, 1966.

Grayson, C. *Leon Battista Alberti: On Painting and On Sculpture: the Latin texts of De Pictura and De Statua edited with English translations, introduction and notes*. London: Phaidon, 1972.

Haber, R. N. Visual perception. *Annual Review of Psychology*, 1978, *29*, 31–59.

Haber, R. N. *The psychology of visual perception*. New York: Holt, Rinehart & Winston, 1980. 2nd ed.

Hagen, M. A., and Elliott, H. B. An investigation of the relationship between viewing conditions and preference for true and modified perspective in adults. *Journal of Experimental Psychology: Human Perception and Performance*, 1976, *2*, 479–90.

Hagen, M. A., and Jones, R. K. Cultural effects in pictorial perception: how many words is one picture really worth? In R. Walk and H. Pick (eds.), *Perception and experience*. New York: Plenum, 1978.

Hammond, J. H. *The camera obscura: a chronicle*. Bristol, England: Adam Hilger, 1981.

Hartt, F. *History of Italian Renaissance art*. Englewood Cliffs, N.J. and New York: Prentice-Hall and Abrams, 1969.

Hatfield, G. C., and Epstein, W. The sensory core and the medieval foundations of early modern perceptual theory. *ISIS*, 1979, *70*, 363–84.

Hauser, A. Space and time in the film. In R. D. MacCann (ed.), *Film: a montage of theories*. New York: Dutton, 1966. Excerpt from A. Hauser's *The social history of art*. New York: Knopf, 1951.

Hershenson, M. Moon illusion and spiral aftereffect: illusions due to the loom-zoom system. *Journal of Experimental Psychology: General*, 1982, *111*, 423–40.

Howard, I. P., *Human visual orientation*. New York: Wiley, 1982.

Huffman, D. A. Impossible objects as nonsense sentences. In B. Meltzer and D. Michie (eds.), *Machine Intelligence 6*. Edinburgh: Edinburgh University Press, 1971.

Ivins, W. M., Jr. *On the rationalization of sight*. New York: Da Capo Press, 1973. First pub. 1938.

Jacobus de Voragine. *The golden legend*. New York: Arno Press, 1969. Trans. and adapted from the Latin by G. Ryan and H. Ripperberger.

Janson, H. W. Ground plan and elevation in Masaccio's *Trinity* fresco. In D. Fraser, H. Hibbard, and M. Lewine (eds.), *Essays presented to R. Wittkower on his sixty-fifth birthday*. London: Phaidon, 1967.

Kaftal, G. *Iconography of the saints in Tuscan painting*. Florence: Sansoni, 1952.

Kaftal, G. *Iconography of the saints in central and south Italian schools of painting*. Florence: Sansoni, 1965.

Kaftal, G. *Iconography of the saints in the painting of north east Italy*. Florence: Sansoni, 1978.

Kaufman, L. and Rock, I. The moon illusion. I. *Science*, 1962, *136*, 953–61.

Kemp, M. Science, non-science, and nonsense: the interpretation of Brunelleschi's perspective. *Art History*, 1978, *1*, 134–61.

Kennedy, J. M. *A psychology of picture perception*. San Francisco: Jossey-Bass, 1974.

Kepes, G. *Language of vision*. Chicago: P. Theobold, 1944.

177

Kitao, T. K. *Imago and pictura:* perspective, camera obscura and Kepler's optics. In M. D. Emiliani (ed.), *La prospettiva rinascimentale: codificazioni e trasgressioni.* Florence: Centro Di, 1980.

Koslow, S. De wonderlijke Perspectyfkas: an aspect of seventeenth-century Dutch painting. *Oud Holland,* 1967, *82,* 35–56.

Kosslyn, S. M. Measuring the visual angle of the mind's eye. *Cognitive Psychology,* 1978, *10,* 356–89.

Krautheimer, R. Brunelleschi and linear perspective. In I. Hyman (ed.), *Brunelleschi in perspective.* Englewood Cliffs, N.J.: Prentice-Hall, 1974. Excerpt from *Lorenzo Ghiberti,* first pub. 1956.

Kristeller, P. O. *Renaissance thought: the classic, scholastic, and humanist strains.* New York: Harper Torchbooks, 1961. First pub. 1955.

Kristeller, P. O. Marsilio Ficino. In P. Edwards (ed.), *Encyclopedia of philosophy.* New York: Macmillan and Free Press, 1967.

Kubovy, M., Turock, D. L., Best, T. L., and Marcus, J. The virtual vantage point for the identification of cutaneous patterns. Unpub.

La Gournerie, J. de. *Traité de perspective linéaire.* Paris: Dalmont et Dunod; Mallet-Bachelier, 1859.

La Gournerie, J. de *Traité de perspective linéaire.* Paris: Gauthier-Villars, 1884. 2d ed.

Lakoff, G., and Johnson, M. *Metaphors we live by.* Chicago: University of Chicago Press, 1981.

Lee, D. N., and Aronson, E. Visual proprioceptive control of standing in human infants. *Perception and Psychophysics,* 1974, *15,* 529–32.

Lee, D. N., and Lishman, J. R. Visual proprioceptive control of stance. *Journal of Human Movement Studies,* 1975, *1,* 87–95.

Leeman, F., Ellfers, E., and Schuyt, M. *Hidden images: games of perception, anamorphic art, illusion.* New York: Abrams, 1976.

Leonardo da Vinci. *The notebooks of Leonardo da Vinci.* Ed. E. MacCurdy. London: Reynal & Hitchcock, 1938.

Leonardo da Vinci. *The literary works of Leonardo da Vinci.* Ed. J. P. Richter. London: Phaidon, 1970.

Liotard, J. E. *Traité des principes et des règles de la peinture.* Geneva: Minkoff Reprint, 1973. First pub. 1781.

Lumsden, E. A. Problems of magnification and minification: an explanation of the distortions of distance, slant, shape, and velocity. In M. A. Hagen (ed.), *The perception of pictures.* Vol. 1: *Alberti's window: the projective model of pictorial information.* New York: Academic Press, 1980.

Lynes, J. A. Brunelleschi's perspectives reconsidered. *Perception,* 1980, *9,* 87–99.

Martin, K. *Chance and order: drawings.* London: Waddington Galleries, 1973. Introduction, A. Forge; notes, H. Lane.

Mastai, M.-L. d'O. *Illusion in art. Trompe l'oeil: a history of pictorial illusionism.* New York: Abaris Books, 1975.

Merleau-Ponty, M. Eye and mind. In *The Primacy of Perception and other essays on phenomenological psychology, and philosophy of art, history and politics.* Evanston, Ill.: Northwestern University Press, 1964. First pub. in French as "L'Oeil et l'esprit," 1961.

Monaco, J. *How to read a film: the art, technology, language, history, and theory of film and media.* New York: Oxford University Press, 1977.

Murray, P., and Murray, L. *The art of the Renaissance.* New York: Praeger, 1963.

Olmer, P. *Perspective artistique.* Vol. 1: *Principes et méthodes.* Paris: Plon, 1943.

Olmer, P. *Perspective artistique.* Vol. 2: *Tracés pratiques.* Paris: Plon, 1949.

Ono, H. On Wells's (1792) law of visual direction. *Perception and Psychophysics*, 1981, *30*, 403–6.

Ono, H. and Comerford, J. Stereoscopic depth constancy. In W. Epstein (ed.), *Stability and constancy in visual perception: mechanisms and processes.* New York: Wiley, 1977.

Pallucchini, P. *La pittura veneziana del Trecento.* Venice, 1964.

Panofsky, E. Die Perspektive als 'symbolische Form'. *Vorträge der Bibliothek Warburg*, 1924/25, *4*, 258–331.

Pastore, N. On Brunelleschi's perspective 'experiments' or demonstrations. *Italian Journal of Psychology*, 1979, *6*, 157–80.

Pastore, N., and Rosen, E. Alberti and the camera obscura. *Physis*, 1984, *26*, 259–69.

Paz, O. *Marcel Duchamp: appearance stripped bare.* New York: Seaver Books, 1981.

Pedretti, C. *Leonardo architetto.* N. p.: Electa, 1978.

Perkins, D. N. Cubic corners. Quarterly Progress Report 89, M.I.T. Research Laboratory of Electronics, 1968, pp. 207–14. (Reprinted in Harvard Project Zero Technical Report no. 5, 1971.)

Perkins, D. N. Visual discrimination between rectangular and nonrectangular parallelepipeds. *Perception and Psychophysics*, 1972, *12*, 396–400.

Perkins, D. N. Compensating for distortion in viewing pictures obliquely. *Perception and Psychophysics*, 1973, *14*, 13–18.

Perkins, D. N., and Cooper, R. G., Jr. How the eye makes up what light leaves out. In M. A. Hagen (ed.), *The perception of pictures.* Vol. 2: *Dürer's devices: beyond the projective model of pictures.* New York: Academic Press, 1980.

Pignatti, T. Introduction. In G. Fiocco (ed.), *The frescoes of Mantegna in the Eremitani Church, Padua.* Oxford: Phaidon, 1978.

Pirenne, M. H. *Optics, painting and photography.* Cambridge: Cambridge University Press, 1970.

Pirenne, M. H. The scientific basis for Leonardo da Vinci's theory of perspective. *British Journal for the Philosophy of Science*, 1952–3, *3*, 169–85.

Pollitt, J. J. *Art and experience in classical Greece.* Cambridge: Cambridge University Press, 1972.

Pope-Hennessy, J. *Paolo Uccello.* 2d ed. London, 1969.

Prager, F. D., and Scaglia, G. *Brunelleschi: studies of his technology and inventions.* Cambridge, Mass.: MIT Press, 1972.

Puppi, L. Il trasferimento del Mantegna a Mantova: una data per l'incontro con l'Alberti. In *Il Sant' Andrea di Mantova e Leon Battista Alberti.* Mantua: Biblioteca Communale, 1974.

Raine, K. *Collected poems.* London: Hamish Hamilton, 1956.

Rock, I. In defense of unconscious inference. In W. Epstein (ed.), *Stability and constancy in visual perception: mechanisms and processes.* New York: Wiley, 1977.

Rock, I. *The logic of perception.* Cambridge, Mass.: Bradford Books and MIT Press, 1983.

Rock, I., and Kaufman, L. The moon illusion. II. *Science,* 1962, *136,* 1023–31.

Roemer, M. The surface of reality. In R. D. MacCann (ed.), *Film: a montage of theories.* New York: Dutton, 1966. First pub. in *Film Quarterly,* 1964, *18,* 15–22.

Rosenberg, H. *The de-definition of art.* New York: Collier, 1973.

Rosinski, R. R., and Farber, J. Compensation for viewing point in the perception of pictured space. In M. A. Hagen (ed.), *The perception of pictures.* Vol. 1: *Alberti's window: the projective model of pictorial information.* New York: Academic Press, 1980.

Rosinski, R. R., Mulholland, T., Degelman, D., and Farber, J. Picture perception: an analysis of visual compensation. *Perception and Psychophysics,* 1980, *28,* 521–6.

Rubin, E. *Synoplevelde figurer.* Copenhagen: Gyldendalske, 1915.

Sanders, A. *The selective process in the functional visual field.* Soesterberg, The Netherlands: Institute for Perception (RVO-TNO), 1963.

Sanpaolesi, P. *Brunelleschi.* N. p.: G. Barbera, 1962.

Santapà F. *Prospettiva su quadro non verticale.* Palermo: Edizioni i.l.a. Palma, 1968.

Schlosberg, H. Stereoscopic depth from single pictures. *American Journal of Psychology,* 1941, *44,* 601–5.

Shepard, R. S. Psychophysical complementarity. In M. Kubovy and J. R. Pomerantz (eds.), *Perceptual organization.* Hillsdale, N.J.: Lawrence Erlbaum, 1981.

Smith, P. C., and Smith, O. W. Ball-throwing responses to photographically portrayed targets. *Journal of Experimental Psychology,* 1961, *62,* 223–33.

Steinberg, L. Leonardo's *Last Supper. Art Quarterly,* 1973, *36,* 297–410.

Stevens, W. *The palm at the end of the mind: selected poems and a play.* New York: Vintage Books, 1972.

Sypher, W. *Four stages of Renaissance style: transformations in art and literature, 1400–1700.* Gloucester, Mass.: Peter Smith, 1978. Reprint of 1954 ed. pub. by Doubleday.

Thom, R. *Structural stability and morphogenesis.* Reading, Mass.: Benjamin, 1975. D. H. Fowler, trans.

Vasari, G. *The lives of the artists.* Harmondsworth, England: Penguin Books, 1965. G. Bull, trans.

Vredeman de Vries, J. *Perspective.* New York: Dover, 1968.

Wallach, H. The apparent rotation of pictorial scenes. In M. Henle (ed.), *Vision and artifact.* New York: Springer, 1976.

Welch, R. B. *Perceptual modification: adapting to altered sensory environments.* New York: Academic Press, 1978.

Welliver, W. The symbolic architecture of Domenico Veneziano and Piero della Francesca. *Art Quarterly,* 1973, *36,* 1–30.

Wells, W. C. *An essay upon single vision with two eyes, together with experiments and observations on several other subjects in optics.* London: T. Cadell, 1792.

Wheatstone, C. Contributions to the physiology of vision.–Part the first. On some remarkable, and hitherto unobserved, phenomena of binocular vision. *Philosophical Transactions of the Royal Society of London,* 1838, [128], 371–94. Excerpts reprinted in W. N. Dember (ed.), *Visual perception: the nineteenth century.* New York: Wiley, 1964.

Wheelock, A. K., Jr. *Perspective, optics, and Delft artists around 1650.* New York: Garland, 1977. Reprint of 1973 Ph.D. dissertation.

White, J. *The birth and rebirth of pictorial space.* Boston: Boston Book and Art Shop, 1967. 2d ed.

Wimsatt, W. K. How to compose chess problems, and why. In J. Ehrmann (ed.), *Game, play, literature.* Boston: Beacon Press, 1968.

Winner, E. *Invented worlds: the psychology of the arts.* Cambridge, Mass.: Harvard University Press, 1982.

Figure acknowledgments and sources

Figure I-1. Andrea Mantegna, *Archers Shooting at Saint Christopher.* Courtesy Alinari/Art Resource, Inc.

Figure I-2. Taddeo Gaddi, *The Presentation of the Virgin.* Courtesy Art Resource, Inc.

Figure I-3. Piero della Francesca, *Flagellation.* Courtesy Soprintendenza per i beni artistici e storici delle Marche, Urbino.

Figure I-4. Masaccio, *Tribute Money.* Courtesy Alinari/Art Resource, Inc.

Figure I-5. Piero della Francesca, *Madonna and Child, Six Saints, Four Angels, and Duke Federico II da Montefeltro.* Courtesy Soprintendenza per i beni artistici e storici, Milan.

Figure I-6. Domenico Veneziano, *Martyrdom of Saint Lucy.* Courtesy Gemäldegalerie, West Berlin.

Figure I-7. Raphael, *Dispute Concerning the Blessed Sacrament.* Courtesy Alinari/Art Resource, Inc.

Figure I-8. Domenico Veneziano, *Madonna and Child with Four Saints.* Courtesy Alinari/Art Resource, Inc.

Figure I-9. Pietro Perugino, *Virgin Appearing to Saint Bernard.* Courtesy Direktion der Bayerischen Staatsgemäldesammlungen.

Figure I-10. Copy after Mantegna, *Archers Shooting at Saint Christopher; Saint James Being Led to Execution; Saint Christopher's Body Being Dragged Away after His Beheading.* Courtesy Musée Jacquemart-André, Paris; photo: Etablissements J. E. Bulloz.

Figure I-11. Andrea Mantegna, *Saint Christopher's Body Being Dragged Away after His Beheading.* Fiocco, 1978, plate XVII; courtesy Phaidon Press Ltd.

Figure I-12. Leon Battista Alberti, Church of San Francesco, Rimini. Photo: Sergio Anelli; courtesy Electa Editrice, Milan.

Figure I-13. Leon Battista Alberti, Church of San Francesco, Rimini. Photo: Sergio Anelli; courtesy Electa Editrice, Milan.

Figure I-14. Andrea Mantegna, detail of Figure I-11. Fiocco, 1978, Plate XXII; courtesy Phaidon Press Ltd.

Figure I-15. Leon Battista Alberti, *Self-portrait.* National Gallery of Art, Washington.

182

Figure 1-1. Masaccio, *Trinity*. Courtesy Art Resource, Inc.

Figure 1-2. Alberti's window. G. B. Vignola, *La due regole della prospettiva practica*. Courtesy Beineke Rare Book and Manuscript Library, Yale University.

Figure 1-3. *Camera obscura*. R. Gemma Frisius, *De radio astronomico et geometrico liber*. By permission of the British Library.

Figure 1-6. *The Flying Fish of Tyre*. Courtesy the Pierpont Morgan Library, New York.

Figure 1-7. Jan van Eyck, *Annunciation*. Courtesy Thyssen-Bornemisza Collection, Lugano, Switzerland.

Figure 1-8. Mantegna, *Martyrdom of Saint James*. Fiocco, 1978, plate XII; courtesy Phaidon Press, Ltd.

Figure 1-11. Plan and elevation of Masaccio's *Trinity*. Sanpaolesi, 1962, Figure C, opp. p. 52; courtesy Istituto Geographico de Agostini, Milan.

Figure 1-13. Leonardo da Vinci, *Alberti's construzione legittima*. Courtesy Bibliotèque de l'Institut, Paris; photo: Etablissements J. E. Bulloz.

Figure 2-1. Brunelleschi's first experiment. Diagram IX-1 from *The Renaissance Rediscovery of Linear Perspective*, by Samuel Y. Edgerton, Jr., copyright 1975 by Samuel Y. Edgerton, Jr.; reprinted by permission of Basic Books, Inc., Publishers.

Figure 3-2. Fra Andrea Pozzo, *Saint Ignatius Being Received into Heaven*. Courtesy Alinari/Art Resource, Inc.

Figure 3-3. Andrea Mantegna, ceiling fresco. Courtesy Soprintendenza per i beni artistici e storici per le provincie di Brescia, Cremona, Mantua; photo: Querci fotografia.

Figure 3-4. Baldassare Peruzzi, fresco. Salla delle Prospettive, Villa Farnesina, Rome. Coffin, 1979, Figure 65, p. 101; by permission Fototeca de Arte Post Antica, Bibliotheca Herziana, Rome.

Figure 3-5. Peruzzi, fresco. Salla delle Prospettive, Villa Farnesina, Rome. Frommel, 1961, Plate Vc; by permission Walter de Gruyter & Co., Berlin.

Figure 3-6. Focus and depth of field. Monaco, 1977, Figure 2-15, pp. 68–9; by permission Oxford University Press, New York.

Figure 4-1. Panels 95, 96, and 97. La Gournerie, *Traité de perspective linéaire*, 1884, Plate 14.

Figure 4-2. Jan Vredeman de Vries, architectural perspective. Vredeman de Vries, 1968, Part II, Figure 22.

Figure 4-5. Experimental data. After Rosinski et al., 1980, Figure 2, p. 523.

Figure 4-6. Experimental data. After Rosinski et al., 1980, Figure 3, p. 523.

Figure 4-7. Experimental data. After Rosinski et al., 1980, Figure 5, p. 525.

Figure 4-8. Pierre-Etienne-Théodore Rousseau, *The Village of Becquigny*. Copyright the Frick Collection, New York.

Figure 4-9. Experimental data. After Goldstein, 1979, Figure 11, p. 85.

Figure 5-3. Carlo Crivelli (attrib.), *Saints Catherine of Alexandria and Mary Magdalene*. Courtesy of the Trustees, The National Gallery, London.

Figure 5-4. Antonello da Messina, *Salvatore Mundi*. Courtesy of the Trustees, The National Gallery, London.

Figure 5-5. Jan van Eyck, *Portrait of a Young Man*. Courtesy of the Trustees, The National Gallery, London.

Figure 5-6. Francisco de Zurbarán, *Saint Francis in Meditation*. Courtesy of the Trustees, The National Gallery, London.

Figure 5-7. Laurent Dabos, *Peace Treaty between France and Spain*. Courtesy Musée Marmottan, Paris; photo: Studio Lourmel 77.

Figure 5-8. French School, *Rome*. Courtesy the Cooper-Hewitt Museum, the Smithsonian Institution's National Museum of Design. Gift of Sara and Eleanor Hewitt.

Figure 5-9. Cornelis Gijsbrechts, *Easel*. Courtesy Statens Museum for Kunst, Copenhagen; photo: Hans Petersen.

Figure 5-10. Jean-Baptiste Chardin, *The White Tablecloth*. Courtesy the Art Institute of Chicago.

Figure 5-11. J. van der Vaart (attrib.), *Painted Violin*. By permission of the Chatsworth Settlement Trustees.

Figure 5-12. Jacopo de'Barbari, *Dead Partridge*. Courtesy Direktion der Bayerischen Staatsgemäldesammlungen.

Figure 5-13. Edward Collier, *Quod Libet*. Courtesy the Victoria and Albert Museum, London.

Figure 5-14. Samuel van Hoogstraten, *Still Life*. Courtesy Gemäldegalerie der Akademie der bildended Künste, Vienna.

Figure 5-15. Wallerant Vaillant, *Four Sides*. Courtesy Galleria Lorenzelli, Bergamo, Italy.

Figure 5-16. Drawing. From Kennedy, 1974, Figure 7, p. 52; by permission of the author and Jossey-Bass Inc.

Figure 5-18. A Necker cube formed by cognitive contours. Reprinted by permission from *Nature*, Vol. 261, No. 5555, pp. 77–8; copyright 1976, Macmillan Journals Ltd.

Figure 6-1. Donatello, *The Feast of Herod*. Courtesy Alinari/Art Resource, Inc.

Figure 6-4. Photograph of a photograph. *Time*, March 29, 1968; courtesy Wide World Photos.

Figure 6-8. Distorted room. Courtesy Institute for Associated Research, Hanover, N.H.

Figure 6-9. Two views of John Hancock Tower, Boston. Courtesy John Hancock Mutual Life Insurance Co.

Figure 6-17. Stimuli for experiment. Shepard, 1981, Figure 10.6, p. 304; by permission of the author and Lawrence Erlbaum Associates, Inc.

Figure 6-18. Experimental data. Shepard, 1981, Figure 10.7, p. 306; by permission of the author and Lawrence Erlbaum Associates, Inc.

Figure 7-1. Two central projections of a church and cloister. Olmer, 1943, Plate 64.

Figure 7-2. Cubes seen under normal perspective. Olmer, 1943, Plate 93.

Figure 7-3. Cubes seen under exaggerated perspective. Olmer, 1943, Plate 95.

Figure 7-4. Marginal distortions in cubes. Olmer, 1943, Plate 98.

Figure 7-6. Experimental data. Sanders, 1963, Figure 6, p. 51; by permission of the author and the Institute for Perception, TNO.

Figure 7-8. Projections on and off the principal ray. Olmer, 1943, Plate 96.

Figure 7-9. Raphael, *The School of Athens*. Courtesy Musei Vaticani.

Figure 7-10. Detail of Figure 7-9. Courtesy Musei Vaticani.

Figure 7-11. Plan of cylindrical columns. La Gournerie, 1884, Figure 202.

Figure 7-12. Paolo Uccello, *Sir John Hawkwood*. Courtesy Alinari/Art Resource, Inc.

Figure 7-13. Diagram. Goodman, 1976, Fig. 1, p. 18; reproduced by permission of Nelson Goodman from *Languages of Art*, Hackett Publishing Co., Inc., Indianapolis.

Figure 8-1. Brunelleschi's second experiment. From *The Renaissance Rediscovery of Linear Perspective*, by Samuel Y Edgerton, Jr., copyright 1975 by Samuel Y. Edgerton, Jr.; reprinted by permission of Basic Books, Inc., Publishers.

Figure 8-3. Kenneth Martin, *Chance and Order Drawing 1981*. Courtesy Ruth and Andrew Forge, New Haven, Conn.

Figure 8-4. Jean Tinguely, *Homage to New York*. Photo: David Gahr.

Figure 8-5. Marcel Duchamp, *Bottlerack*. Courtesy The Museum of Modern Art, New York.

Figure 8-6. Advertisement. Courtesy Warner Co.

Figure 8-7. Andrea Mantegna, *Saint James Led to Execution*. Fiocco, 1978, Plate X; courtesy Phaidon Press Ltd.

Figure 8-9. Leonardo da Vinci, *The Last Supper*. Courtesy Soprintendenza per i beni artistici e storici, Milan.

Figure 8-10. Analysis of perspective construction of Leonardo's *Last Supper*. Pedretti, 1978, Figure 428, p. 287, bottom panel; drawing: Giovanni Degl'Innocenti; courtesy Electa Editrice, Milan.

Figure 8-11. Reconstructed plan and longitudinal elevation of room represented in Leonardo's *Last Supper*. Pedretti, 1978, Figure 426, p. 286, bottom panel; drawing: Giovanni Degl'Innocenti; courtesy Electa Editrice, Milan.

Figure 8-12. Leonardo's *Last Supper*. Photograph taken from a height of 4.5 m. Courtesy Soprintendenza per i beni artistici e storici, Milan.

Figure 8-13. Steinberg's cardboard model. Courtesy Professor Leo Steinberg.

Figure 8-14. Cropped version of Figure 8-9.

Figure 8-15. Cropped version of Figure 8-9.

Figure 9-1. Definitions of two elementary camera movements: pan and tilt. Monaco, 1977, two left-side panels of Figure 2-22, p. 78; by permission Oxford University Press.

Figure 9-2. The moving room of Lee and Aronson (1974)

Figure 9-4. The Parthenon, from northwest. Courtesy Alinari/Art Resource, Inc.

Figure 9-5. Diagram of Parthenon. Pollitt, 1972, Figure 32, p. 77; courtesy Cambridge University Press.

Figure 10-1. Paolo Uccello, *Perspective Study of a Chalice*. Courtesy Alinari/Art Resource, Inc.

Figure 10-2. Sol LeWitt, untitled (1969). Courtesy John Weber Gallery, New York.

Figure 10-3. Leonardo da Vinci, *A War Machine* (Codex Atlanticus, Folio 387ʳ). Courtesy Art Resource, Inc.

Figure 10-4. Kasimir Malevich: *Suprematist Elements: Two Squares* (1913); *Suprematist Element: Circle* (1913). Courtesy Museum of Modern Art, New York.

Figure 10-5. Piero della Francesca (attrib. doubtful), *Perspective of an Ideal City*. Courtesy Soprintendenza per i beni artistici e storici delle Marche, Urbino.

Figure 10-6. Gentile Bellini, *Procession of the Relic of the True Cross*. Courtesy Alinari/Art Resource, Inc.

Index